THE UNIVERSITY OF CHICAGO STUDIES
IN LIBRARY SCIENCE

PUBLISHERS AND LIBRARIANS

PUBLISHERS AND LIBRARIANS
A Foundation for Dialogue

*Proceedings of the Forty-second Conference
of the Graduate Library School,
May 13–15, 1983*

Edited by MARY BIGGS

THE UNIVERSITY OF CHICAGO PRESS
Chicago and London

THE UNIVERSITY OF CHICAGO STUDIES IN LIBRARY SCIENCE

*The papers in this volume were published originally
in the LIBRARY QUARTERLY,
January 1984*

THE UNIVERSITY OF CHICAGO PRESS, CHICAGO 60637
THE UNIVERSITY OF CHICAGO PRESS, LTD., LONDON

Library of Congress Cataloging in Publication Data
Main entry under title:

Publishers and librarians.

   Includes bibliographical references.
   1. Libraries and publishing—Congresses.   2. Library
science—Congresses.   3. Publishers and publishing—
Congresses.   I. Biggs, Mary.   II. University of Chicago.
Graduate Library School.
Z716.6.P83   1984   025.2   83-18124
ISBN 0-226-04846-2
ISBN 0-226-04847-0 (pbk.)

CONTENTS

.

INTRODUCTION[1]

Mary Biggs[2]

The nature, history, and current concerns and practices of the publishing industry have always been centrally important to the Graduate Library School—an importance evidenced by its curriculum and the research of its faculty and students, as well as by several previous conferences (see, for example, [1–3]). That this should be so may seem as unsurprising as that attorneys should be interested in the legislative process or physicians in medical research. But are they? Or is the law as accomplished fact, the treatment or drug as developed tool, often the practitioner's exclusive preoccupation? Is the book (or periodical or recording or microform or computer program) as a finished, perhaps troublesome, costly product—to be purchased or not, processed or not, and if so, how and why—usually the librarian's sole focus?

The Graduate Library School's forty-second conference was built on the assumption that this is the case—that many librarians have misconceptions, or no conception, about the operations, problems, and prospects of the industry responsible for disseminating, in permanent form, the new knowledge and original thought it is the librarian's mission to make accessible. In mid-1982, when conference planning began, librar-

1. On behalf of the Graduate Library School, I wish to thank the Council on Library Resources for providing support that made the Forty-second Conference possible.
2. Bowling Green State University Library, Information Services, Bowling Green, Ohio 43403.

1

ies and publishing houses were both suffering stress brought on by a weakened economy, reordered national political priorities, changed social emphases, and galloping technological progress accompanied by futile resistance on the one hand and foolish over-optimism on the other. It seemed advisable, therefore, to bring members of the two communities together for discussion of their common problems from their different perspectives.

A majority of speakers was drawn from among publishers and editors concerned with original scholarship and serious creative literature, the types of material most crucial to research libraries and most dependent on purchase by them. The sciences, social sciences, and humanities were represented, and both the for-profit and nonprofit sectors. Invited to respond to the publishers were two research librarians: Jay Lucker, who heads a primarily scientific and technical library, and Charles Osburn, a humanist with expertise in collection development. The opening and final speakers were Lewis A. Coser and Lester Asheim, university faculty members distinguished at once by their distance from publishing and library practice and by their intellectual involvement with them.

Speakers representing the publishing industry were given a wide-ranging list of subjects for contemplation, but none was assigned a specific topic or even restricted to the list. Instead, each was charged with identifying those matters he or she deemed most significant and most critical for librarians to understand. The responding librarians, likewise, were not asked to address the publishers' arguments point by point but rather to select particularly captivating aspects for analysis. The speakers' choices of emphasis are, then, revealing in themselves—and their direct clashes, their harmonies, and their sometimes striking dovetails, are particularly interesting.

Sounding a note that reverberates throughout this volume, Frederick Praeger insists that "we cannot permit the book to drown in electronic tidal waves" and demands, "Can we take our cathode ray tube to bed? Can we write in its margins? Can we comfortably rest and reflect or flip back and forth in a pile of printouts?" [4, pp. 29, 25–26]. While conceding cathode ray tubes' unattractiveness as bed partners, Peter Urbach points out that "neither can you take the many bound volumes of the case law of the state of Illinois or the hard copy of the Chemical Abstract Service to bed" [5, p. 32]. A lawyer and electronic publishing specialist, Urbach veers sharply from this volume's prevailing view with his characterization of publisher-librarian interactions as a "zero-sum game" rendering "dialogue" essentially pointless and finally unneeded: "The future of these difficulties will be resolved by advances in the technology" [5, p. 32].

Other authors, however, cite technology's continuing and probably increasing exacerbation of conflict through its facilitation of copying, resource sharing, publishing proliferousness, and the relinquishment, by both book and journal editors, of their traditional quality-control functions. (On the other hand, some of these same authors anticipate that progress in production automation may permit lower prices—to everyone's delight.) Several call for more publisher-librarian gatherings to help smooth differences, if not always resolve them. Far from viewing the two communities as hostages in a zero-sum game, they imply a symbiosis, in which one cannot lose without the other losing and inflicting the gravest, most irrecoverable loss of all on the larger society both groups are committed to serve.

Representing another and less often considered perspective, Bill Henderson and Ted Solotaroff write as advocates of the poet and fictioneer whose work is meritorious but unlikely to win wide audiences. Heavily dependent on library acquisitions for its meager sales and threatened, as are scholarly and technical works, by economic strain in higher education, creative literature is jeopardized further, Solotaroff claims, by social disregard and by the organizational changes and sharpened sensitivity to profit that have characterized publishing in recent decades.

Indeed, while the dark shadow (or shady relief) of advancing technology dominates several of these papers, a second separate but related theme is also notable for its recurrence: the tension felt by publishers between "commerce and culture," in Coser's terminology [6, p. 9]; "market value" and "intrinsic value," in Morris Philipson's [7, p. 14]; or the "publishing culture and the literary culture," in Solotaroff's [8, p. 73]. Drawing parallels with librarianship, Osburn speaks of "service" versus "collection building" [9, p. 82], Asheim of the library's need to win a certain measure of popular support and at the same time function as conscientious cultural guardian [10].

The drive for profit (or relief from costs) even at some expense to fundamental mission and the drive to exploit technology for gain arise, of course, from the same motive and are shared by publishers and librarians. They are, furthermore, not only understandable but entirely to be expected: "Can publishers really expect libraries to turn away from their elegant electronic interlibrary loan systems and once again begin to purchase multiple copies?" asks Urbach [5, p. 35], and can librarians expect publishers to react favorably?

While there is basis for empathy, then, in shared stresses, motivations, and purpose, librarians still seek to reduce costs of materials purchase (sometimes insensible or careless of the long-range damage thus inflicted) and publishers still seek to extract libraries' dollars (sometimes ignorant or callous about how few and how strained those dollars are). When it is ignorance, confusion, or misinterpretation that has engendered conflict, frank dialogue *can* bear fruit. And it is this kind of dialogue, in this context, that the Graduate Library School hoped to foster through its forty-second conference.

REFERENCES

1. Asheim, Lester, and Fenwick, Sara I., eds. *Differentiating the Media.* Chicago: University of Chicago Press, 1975.
2. Swanson, Don R., ed. *The Role of Libraries in the Growth of Knowledge.* Chicago: University of Chicago Press, 1980.
3. Sutherland, Zena, ed. *Children in Libraries: Patterns of Access to Materials and Services in Schools and Public Libraries.* Chicago: University of Chicago Press, 1981.
4. Praeger, Frederick A. "Librarians, Publishers, and Scholars, Common Interests, Different Views: The View of an Independent Scholarly Publisher." In this issue.
5. Urbach, Peter F. "The View of a For-Profit Scientific Publisher." In this issue.
6. Coser, Lewis A. "The Publishing Industry as a Hybrid." In this issue.
7. Philipson, Morris. "Intrinsic Value versus Market Value." In this issue.
8. Solotaroff, Ted. "The Publishing Culture and the Literary Culture." In this issue.
9. Osburn, Charles B. "Issues of Structure and Control in the Scholarly Communication System." In this issue.
10. Asheim, Lester. "The Foundation for the Dialogue." In this issue.

THE PUBLISHING INDUSTRY AS A HYBRID

Lewis A. Coser[1]

The publishing industry is a hybrid not only because it encompasses firms of very different sizes, with dissimilar market relations and types of products, but also because the operating procedures of individual firms have features that are usually found in bureaucratic enterprises at the same time as they have characteristics usually found in industries built on craftlike enterprises. Some of its centralized operating procedures are similar, for example, to those in the automobile industry, while others resemble the construction industry with its loose coordination of a great variety of individual decisions. The hybrid character of the industry makes for a great deal of inefficiency, but it also affords an opportunity to temper concern for the bottom line with attention to books which, while they may not be profitable, serve our common culture. Hence concern for commerce and culture may coexist even though in an environment marked by much inner tension.

Social scientists in general and sociologists in particular have a vested interest in typologies. They are satisfied when they succeed in reducing the diversity of the data with which they wish to deal to some manageable order by establishing typologies that attempt to capture the essential features of phenomena to be discussed. They aim at disregarding, at least initially, specific and peculiar facets of the data so as to bring out main aspects. Thus, political sociologists might talk about pluralistic as distinct from authoritarian regimes, students of religious phenomena may wish to distinguish churches from sects, and students of labor may find it useful to distinguish primary from secondary labor markets.

The commercial publishing industry (I shall not deal with nonprofit publishing) resists typologies which cannot easily capture the industry's contradictory features. Is it a kind of modern cottage industry or is it rather a highly bureaucratized enterprise? It happens to be both. A few

1. Department of Sociology, State University of New York at Stony Brook, Stony Brook, New York 11790.

5

particulars about publishing illustrate the difficulty of characterizing it typologically.

The industry had total sales of $7.039 billion in 1980, which makes it a fairly large, although by no means a top, industry. But, as distinct from other industries of that size, it is highly fragmented into a great number of companies. There are some fifteen thousand publishers having books in print, but most of these publish only a handful of books each year. Capital requirements are very low, so almost anyone can try his or her hand at publishing. The leading houses, of which there are no more than about fifty, may be lodged in gleaming skyscrapers, in offices that are hardly distinguishable from the headquarters of other major corporations. But small publishers may operate from a few rented rooms or even from the private home of the publisher. The industry as a whole comprises at the same time the equivalents of Howard Johnson and the mom-and-pop delicatessen store. It is fragmented into a variety of firms that differ in size, operating procedures, and relations to the market. Even more important, the internal operations in particular firms also exhibit peculiar characteristics that make it impossible to classify even its major firms unambiguously as bureaucratic enterprises similar to those in other industrial or commercial sectors.

To be sure, bureaucratic characteristics have become more pronounced in the last two decades of the industry's development and have partially replaced more individualized and particularistic features. Old-time editors will regale the researcher with stories about the golden days of the past when personal criteria, individual taste, and a sense of cultural responsibility governed decisions to sign or not to sign a book contract. However, there is always a strong element of nostalgia in such accounts—one wonders whether even in the past the industry was really dominated by gentlemen publishers relatively unconcerned with the bottom line—and, even in the age of corporate takeovers, computerized operating procedures, and preponderant concern with blockbusters and media tie-ins, decision making in the world of publishing differs considerably from, say, decision making in the automobile industry. This is not due to happenstance but to the structural characteristics of publishing.

In the typical bureaucratized corporation, key decisions are made on top and then are slowly filtered down to lower levels of the hierarchy. In the automobile industry, for example, key executives will decide whether in the years to come models in a particular line should be constructed, say, in terms of fuel economy or whether, instead, stress should be put on features that increase glamor at the expense of economy. Such decisions once taken will then govern the multitude of minor decisions that have to be made by executives and administrators lower down on the decision-making ladder. While company officials on the lower rank of the hierarchy are by no means automatons and may well propose specific lines of action within their spheres of competence, the operation of the whole firm is largely determined by lines set down on top executive levels. These procedures have become possible in mass-production industries because of the high degree of standardization. No key decisions have to be made in regard to this or that particular automobile that rolls down the assembly line. A central decision, once made, governs the individual product no matter whether 50,000 or 500,000 cars of a particular model will be produced during a given year.

But in the publishing industry such standardized procedures are almost entirely inapplicable. Each book must be handled individually, and hence standardization has narrow limits. As a consequence, while top management may make certain overall decisions as to budget allocation, markets to be addressed, type of books to be published, or profit maximization, decisions as to whether to publish this or that particular book must be delegated to editors and editors-in-chief who are not part of the top administrative hierarchy. In this respect, despite all bureaucratized features, publishing, even in the largest houses, has more in common with a craft industry, such as construction and its only loosely coordinated operations, than with mass industries that are organized along bureaucratic lines [1].

But even the analogy with the construction industry, where, as in publishing, many decisions must be taken fairly low down the line, has only limited utility. As distinct from construction where a building is typically constructed for a known client, publishing, with the exception of textbook publishing, produces for a market that is largely unknown. Nobody really knows whether a given book, except those by some well-established authors, will or will not sell. The industry, again with the exception of textbook publishing, hardly conducts any market research. As a result, most publishing decisions are based on guesswork. When we asked editors or editors-in-chief why they published or refused to publish a book, we invariably got vague answers, such as, "I know it by the seat of my pants" [2]. Certain editors may have better track records than others, but they cannot explain why this is so except by reference to intuition. By and large, decisions cannot be justified by unambiguous criteria.

Market uncertainties are central not only in regard to signing a book contract but also when it comes to pricing the books. The *New York Times Book Review* [3] recently reported that when paperback publishers were asked about the great variety in the price of more or less similar books, Jack Romanos, publisher of Bantam Books, said: "Almost everything we're doing when we price a book is instinctive." Thus the paperback edition of a new book by the popular author John Jakes, *North and South*

[4], will sell for $4.95 while the same author's *The Bastard* [5] now sells at $1.95, having been reduced from $3.95. Pricing decisions are usually based on a great variety of factors, including editorial, advertising, production, and marketing costs, but an intuitive sense of what the market will bear is likely to be as determining as these factors.

Given the unpredictability and fickleness of the market, publishers attempt various methods to reduce uncertainty. They may, for example, tailor products for a relatively predictable group of consumers. Hence the endless series of Gothic novels or western adventures where each book, often the product of regular novel factories which produce non-books by assembly-line methods, resembles the next like one pea resembles another. But such standardization is possible only in a mercifully limited sector of the total market. Large advertising campaigns, appearance of authors on talk shows, and all the other ballyhoo that attends much modern trade publishing, is likewise designed to reduce uncertainty. But, alas, it sometimes works and it sometimes does not.

There is only one branch of publishing, the production of textbooks, that is less plagued by uncertainty. Elementary and high school textbooks are not ordered by individual teachers but by school districts or even on a state level so that market research, given the relatively restricted number of persons who make decisions to adopt a particular textbook, becomes feasible. Similarly, given that college texts are not adopted by the final consumers, the students, but by their teachers, market research among the limited number of teachers is not only feasible but has become the rule in recent years.

The uncertainties of the market for trade books are multiplied by the inefficient, costly, and cumbersome distribution system. Hardcover trade books and mass paperbacks are distributed in a different manner, through bookstores in the first case and through outlets such as drugstores, newspaper stores, airport newsstands, and the like in the second. But what they have in common is the so-called return privilege. In both cases, when a store orders books the sale is not final; the store has the privilege of returning unsold books during a specified period. (In the case of paperbacks not the whole book but only the cover is returned.) Indeed, between 25 percent and 40 percent of all hardcover trade books are returned. For mass paperbacks the figure for returned covers is as high as 50 percent. I know of no other industry which, in order to clear the market, has to destroy half or nearly half its output. The publishing industry has often attempted to modify or to do away with the return privilege, but it has always run into the reaction that without it, a high proportion of the roughly thirteen thousand bookstores, most of which are undercapitalized, would close their doors.

The recent phenomenal growth of book chains can be seen as an attempt to rationalize the distribution of trade books. Chains have been very successful. In the near future almost one-third of trade-book sales to individuals will have been preempted by the chains. The chains with their national outlets have computerized accounting, inventory control, and invoicing. But, above all, they now can provide publishers with detailed information as to what particular type of book sells in what area, to what kind of customer. Even though the chains also enjoy return privileges, they nevertheless have allowed publishers to tailor their print runs to demand in a manner that was not possible beforehand. Presently, publishers may even show book manuscripts or galleys to the major chain store buyers before publication to find out whether their books will find ready markets. This has indeed contributed to the reduction of uncertainty but, and this is of the utmost importance for those of us who are concerned with the contributions books make to our common culture, chains are interested only in books that are likely to be best-sellers. They tend to ignore books that can sell only, or are perceived as likely to sell only, a limited number of copies. As a result, first novels have become so risky from the publisher's point of view that they have faced increasing publisher resistance.

To sum up: book publishing is inherently a risky enterprise given the uncertainty of the market. Recent attempts to decrease uncertainty have largely contributed to concentration on best-sellers, blockbusters, and mass-produced nonbooks. To the extent that the publishing industry attempts to operate like any other industry, it fails to live up to its cultural responsibilities. Book publishing was always perilously poised between the demands of commerce and culture; but the dangers now loom large that commerce and the bottom line will take the upper hand completely.

That a number of publishing houses in recent years have been bought up by huge conglomerates in the entertainment industry is no longer news, and I shall not dwell on this trend here except to remark that to the extent that the corporate parent attempts to control the publishing strategies of its offspring, the results have been disturbing. There were, to be sure, certain positive results of corporate mergers. The infusion of new capital has sometimes led to better working conditions for editors and other personnel. What is more, in certain cases the availability of corporate funds has enabled editors to be somewhat more venturesome in their decision making by sometimes daring to publish books that they might not have published under more stringent financial conditions. But as a whole, corporate takeovers have surely encouraged more attention to the bottom line than would otherwise have been the case.

I have so far limited myself to trade-book publishing, except for a few remarks on textbook sales. Most people unacquainted with publishing

assume that the publication of trade books is its major business. This is
by no means the case. While trade books may be the most publicly visible
line of its products, they are overshadowed in terms of sales both by
textbooks and professional books and monographs. In addition, there
are many other specialized areas of publishing, such as juvenile books,
art books, and works of reference. This remarkable heterogeneity makes
it even more difficult to generalize about *the* book publishing industry.
In fact, anybody who attempts to make statements about *the* industry
automatically disqualifies himself as a serious commentator. Each sector
of the industry operates in a distinct environment, has different relations to the market, different distribution techniques, and even different
types of personnel. The size of print runs, the chances of new authors
breaking in, the capital requirements, and many other factors make for
highly significant differences between sectors. Thus, professional books
and monograph books are not sold in general bookstores but largely
through mail advertisement to scholars and professionals. Since they are
usually high priced and also avoid the discounts that must be granted to
bookstores, they can be published in much smaller print runs and still
yield some profit. While trade books will usually have to sell around
5,000 copies in order to break even, a monograph might turn out a small
profit even with runs as low as 1,000 copies or less. Or, just to pick out at
random another major difference between professional and trade
books, the opinion of salespeople, who must make their pitch to the
booksellers whom they visit, and are key opinion makers in trade publishing, have no relevance for professional books and monographs. Most
of these books are sold directly to customers without intermediaries.
There are many other significant differences that my coauthors and I
have attempted to analyze in our recently published *Books: The Culture
and Commerce of Publishing* [2].

Rather than give further details here, let me dwell on an especially
interesting trend in trade publishing that has assumed major propor-
tions in the last few decades: the phenomenal growth of what is usually
called subsidiary rights. At present, a good number of trade houses
would probably have to go out of business without these subsidiary
rights, such as foreign translation, book club sales, paperback rights, and
sales to television and movie companies. This is a situation hardly paral-
leled in any other industry I can think of. The sales of by-products have
assumed such saliency that they surpass in many cases the profits from
the main operation, that is, the publication of hardcover trade books.

Incidentally, this recent development has had a most interesting effect
on the sexual division of labor in the publishing industry. As long as
subsidiary rights were limited mainly to some meager profits from translations, reprints, and the like, subsidiary rights departments were typi-

cally staffed by women who were traditionally assigned the less re-munerative and less prestigious jobs in the publishing world. But now, given the enormous expansion of the paperback reprint market, and the no less phenomenal growth of movie and television tie-ins, subsidiary rights have often become the proverbial tail that wags the publishing dog. As a result, women who have long specialized in that area have risen to prominence in publishing firms. We have been told several times that people in subsidiary rights, who often auction off best-sellers for huge sums of money to reprinters and the entertainment industry, have become more powerful in many houses than even the editor-in-chief. It is an open question whether in the future men, who used to disdain subsidiary rights positions, will try to muscle in or whether women will successfully defend this newly found turf.

Let me return in my concluding remarks to the comparison between the automobile and the publishing industries. I stated that in publishing, as distinct from the making of cars, each individual product must be separately considered since there are no standardized mass-produced model lines. I believe that it is this peculiar characteristic which allows the industry to be partly freed from the exclusive emphasis on profitability that governs conduct in most other businesses. To be sure, on one level, the publishing business does not differ from any other business. Any firm, be it in cheese processing or publishing, is con-strained by the forces of the market to look at sales and profit. But, and this seems to me of the highest importance, in publishing it is by no means necessary that every particular book bring in a profit. As a leading publisher put it in an interview:

> I don't think we ever turn something down because it is going to lose money. We know that half our books are not going to make money. My theory is: let people look at the results. I don't want to be judged on a book-by-book basis. If we are not making enough money, or no one likes us, then I am doing a bad job. If at the end of the year enough books have made themselves felt and heard, and we have come out ahead financially, everything is fine. How I got there is my own business. So far I got away with it. [6]

There are, to be sure, many firms where profitability alone provides the guiding criteria. Other firms, however, while not being able to be oblivious to the forces of the market, operate along different criteria. They see themselves as responsible not only to stockholders, investors, or private owners but also to the educated public, the common reader, and the community of intellectuals and scholars. It is such firms that take advantage of the structurally hybrid character of publishing to serve the production of significant cultural products even while they cannot be oblivious to the demands of the marketplace. Publishers who make their decisions mainly in terms of the market, be it the market for their books, or the stock market for their shares, respond to real or alleged trends in a largely passive manner. In doing this they elude their cultural responsibility. It is only if and when they are prepared to buck trends, at least for a significant number of the books they publish, that they assume full stature as molders of culture.

Certain structuralist and neo-Marxist approaches to cultural phenomena have tended in recent years to explain them without reference to human agency. People are simply seen, to speak in the language of Louis Althusser and other structural Marxists, as bearers of modes of production, rather than as living human beings. I agree with Harold Garfinkel that such an approach treats people as "cultural dopes" [7, p. 68]. Granted that people operate within the limits of a variety of constraints, the market being a major example of such constraints, there remains a domain of choices that involves the possibility, as the British sociologist Anthony Giddens has put it, of "doing otherwise."

As long as the publishing industry allows at least some of its key members to "do otherwise" than the market would seem to dictate, at least some sectors of the industry will be able to serve our common culture, and such fragile plants as volumes of poetry or experimental first novels will still find a fertile soil. Under such circumstances, the publishing industry will remain a hybrid in which cultural saints and sinners will coexist in precarious, though often antagonistic, cooperation.

REFERENCES

1. Stinchcombe, Arthur. "Bureaucratic and Craft Administration of Production: A Comparative Study." *Administrative Science Quarterly* 4 (September 1959): 168–87.
2. Coser, Lewis A.; Kadushin, Charles; and Powell, Walter W. *Books: The Culture and Commerce of Publishing.* New York: Basic Books, 1982.
3. Appelbaum, Judith. "Paperback Talk: The Price Complex." *New York Times Book Review* (January 30, 1983), p. 31.
4. Jakes, John. *North and South.* New York: Dell Publishing Co., 1983.
5. Jakes, John. *The Bastard.* New York: Jove Publications, 1978.
6. Coser, Lewis A. "The Private and Public Responsibilities of the American Publisher." In *Responsibilities of the American Book Community,* edited by John Y. Cole. Washington, D.C.: Library of Congress, 1981.
7. Garfinkel, Harold. *Studies in Ethnomethodology.* Englewood Cliffs, N.J.: Prentice-Hall, Inc., 1967.

INTRINSIC VALUE VERSUS MARKET VALUE

Morris Philipson[1]

Both the publisher and the librarian undertake seriously "to make new knowledge and significant thought available to the public." But they seek to accomplish these tasks by means of different principles of selection, and this makes for potential conflict. The librarian must select works he feels are worthwhile for his library. The publisher must select works significant for his list. Here economics enters the equation; for the significance of a work in publishing terms must be defined according to its so-called intrinsic value as a scholarly work *combined with* its market value. Publishers are not clairvoyant; "significance" cannot be known in advance. Publishers must price their books in advance of such evaluations. They depend on certain formulae in calculating a work's list price. These formulae are influenced by advances in technology, such as computerized typesetting devices which have the potential for reducing manufacturing costs but whose very newness implies that much of the so-called cost cutting is at this stage experimental. All this data would make the publishing industry seem an economic lottery; to some extent it is.

As the director of the University of Chicago Press, I am the head of a nonprofit scholarly publishing house; but I do not have a head for prophecy and will not pretend to any prediction about what changes are inevitable for the future. As a matter of fact, I have to confess uncertainty about the present. Mysteries abound, even in matters imagined to be factual, let alone issues of interpretation. We cannot be certain of where we are going in the future, and we are not all that sure of where we are at present.

For example, most of us here might be accused of assuming that the statistical facts are known regarding answers to simple questions, such as, How many books were published last year in the United States? or, How many bookstores are there in the United States? While there is a hard center of answers to such questions as, What is a publisher? What is a book? and What is a bookstore? around the margin of each there is

1. University of Chicago Press, 5801 Ellis Avenue, Chicago, Illinois 60637.

13

considerable vagueness. Depending on whose definition is used, different statistics will result. Incidentally, I am not sure there are not problems of definition to answer the question, What is a library? as well. Such
uncertainty of meaning makes dialogue difficult.

Well, then, if there is to be useful conversation between publishers and
research librarians—the dialogue referred to in the title of this conference—I would hope to examine some of the terms that publishers use,
because, to begin with, I am not sure that we speak the same language.
And if we do not learn each others' language, we can only speak past
each other instead of engaging in a dialogue.

The introduction to the prospectus describing this conference begins
with the following declaration: "The publishing and research library
communities share one basic goal: to make new knowledge and
significant thought available to the public." It goes on to say, "This
mutual interdependency, combined with the fact that each community
also has goals and problems unique to itself, has sometimes led to
antagonism and misunderstanding." I assume that these can be characterized by two opposing attitudes, namely, the publisher's question to
libraries, Why don't you buy more of our books and journals? as con-
trasted to the librarian's question, Why do you go on publishing so much
(that we do not have room for) and at prices increasingly higher (that we
do not have funds for)? There may in fact be some misunderstanding on
the part of each, but I suspect the antagonism is clearer than the
misunderstanding.

It would be a foolish publisher who did not believe that everything he
publishes is worthwhile. But then I suppose librarians would say it would
be a very foolish librarian indeed who thought that everything that is
published is worthwhile for his library. So it seems to me that the essence
of the conflict lies in the differences between the principles of selection
operating in the two different camps. Publishers select what they believe
to be most appropriate for their lists; librarians select what they believe
most appropriate for their clients.

What the scholarly publisher and the research librarian have in common is their sense of seriousness about what they do. Based on their
experience and on taking correct advice, they each select for their own
purposes those books which give them some sense of achieving their
goals as they see it "to make new knowledge and significant thought
available to the public." But even that apparently faultless statement,
which we might all agree to on the surface, contains a mystery. The
unanswerable question for the publisher *in advance* of bringing out a
work of "new knowledge" is the estimation of just how "significant" it
might become. What this uncertainty has embodied in it, from the
publisher's point of view, is the question of the relationship between the
so-called intrinsic value of a scholarly work and its market value.

The opposite of "significant" is "trivial," as expressed, with irritation, in the rhetorical question, Why do you publish so many books of "limited" appeal? Or such highly specialized monographs that sell at unreasonably high prices and get used by a faculty member or a student once every three years? I am sure that all of you know the kind of book that is thus caricatured: a 400-page translation of a hitherto unknown Urdu epic poem; a careful study of the parallels between Nietzsche's *Thus Spake Zarathustra* and Saul Bellow's *Henderson the Rain King*; the kind of sociological work which shows that people in professions resulting in high income have higher social prestige than people in professions earning lower incomes—studies in the social sciences that are referred to as making the obvious inescapable.

In contrast, everyone takes pride in an original work of scholarship that appeals to, and comes to be valued by, a sizable number of people— that is, in the intellectual and scholarly world, the equivalent of the best-seller in the world of popular nonfiction. So one step further along that line of thought might be to ask university presses to publish *only* outstanding books of that sort—just as it would be to propose that a commercial publisher publish only best-sellers. But the fact is, no publisher is so prescient as to know which of the many good books that he publishes will become a "great" book. Scholarly publishers are inevitably confronted by the proposals of editors who recommend publication on the so-called intrinsic value of a book, the value it might have to a scholar in a specialized field—regardless of what it will cost to produce or to buy—in effect, regardless of its market considerations. More often than not, in order to keep the list price down to a reasonable or attractive figure, a larger quantity is printed than in the future proves to be the number of copies that is bought, that is, needed, in the marketplace, thus resulting in a financial loss to the publisher.

At this point let me explain how the list price of a book is established.

It seems to me that most people outside of publishing houses— including even librarians and booksellers—labor under the misconception that it is the length of the book that determines its price, and so they say with indignation, How can it be possible that a book of 230 pages costs $35.00?—especially when a popular novel of 380 pages has a list price of $15.00. The truth is that the list price of a book is determined by the relationship among the costs of composition—that is to say, the amount of money invested in typesetting for each page, the number of pages, and the size of the first printing. All three of those costs must be spread over, divided among, shared by, the number of copies that the publisher will invest in—whether, considering the constraints under which he is publishing, he imagines it will take one year or three years or five years to sell out that first printing. Now the cost of composition per page will be the same whether a publisher is bringing out 1,000 copies of a book or 50,000 copies of a book, but the total for composition cost spread over 1,000 copies will result in a price proportionally much higher than that of the 400-page novel where the per-page composition cost is spread over 50,000 copies. As everything that goes into bookmaking becomes more expensive, from salaries and other overhead costs to paper, printing, and binding costs, as well as composition, I see no immediate end to the inflation of list prices. There exists one possible exception—a hope!—that the new technology permitting transferral of typescript from floppy discs or other computer-generated sources to magnetic tapes for photocomposition may well gradually reduce the current cost of composition. But there are many drawbacks to this. Many obstacles have yet to be overcome, and the savings are yet to be steadily realized.

The major obstacle that I refer to is the incompatibility of different technical systems. Authors today are producing manuscripts on word processors, microcomputers, minicomputers, and mainframe computers. Typesetters who have computerized phototypesetting equipment can accept magnetic tape, provided that the tape is prepared in a prespecified, usable way. Discs are more troublesome. One can no more use a disc on a computerized typesetting system than one can play a phonograph record on a tape recorder. An extra step is added to the production process whenever manuscripts come in on discs: it is necessary to transfer (convert) the magnetic manuscript from the discs to a tape. The storage pattern of a disc is controlled by the internal programming of the manufacturer's system and is intended to insure a captive market for each maker's equipment. Discs produced by different manufacturers—and even different models of their own equipment—require separate programs for conversion to magnetic tape. This wildly irrational situation honors the ingenuity of competitors in a free enterprise market and tends to drive publishers crazy. Nevertheless, the number of books produced in magnetic form has increased dramatically over the past three years. From the records of the University of Chicago Press alone I can attest to the fact that the increase has been from 3 books so produced in 1981 to 18 in 1983. In the instance of 1 volume which involved the preparation of a huge number of statistical charts and tables, using the Xerox 9700 resulted in a saving in typesetting costs of $20,000. In consequence, the book is published at a list price of $37.50 rather than $75.00.

In light of the distinction between the editorial judgment of the intrinsic value of a manuscript and the market value judgment that, more often than not, overestimates the number of copies that will be sold in a given period of time, there are very happy exceptions in the opposite direction.

I can give you the example of a work in cultural history that Chicago took on from a young member of the Yale University faculty only after the Yale University Press had declined to publish the book. It is the work entitled *Christianity, Social Tolerance, and Homosexuality: Gay People in Western Europe from the Beginning of the Christian Era to the Fourteenth Century* [1]. It radically challenges the accepted ideas of the past eight hundred years. It is very scholarly indeed and heavily footnoted not only in English but also in French, German, Spanish, Italian, Latin, Greek, Arabic, Hebrew, and Aramaic. It was long, promised to be expensive, and the assumed market was small. Even with outside subsidy to contribute toward the manufacturing costs, the list price was $27.50 on a first printing of 2,500 copies. But, once it appeared, the book received the most remarkable laudatory reviews, not only in scholarly journals but in trade publications such as the *New York Times Book Review* [2], and sales soared. By the end of the first year of publication some 17,000 copies had been sold, and the book won the American Book Award for history that year. It goes on selling at the rate of 6,000 copies each year, now that it is in a paperback edition at $9.95. This is a case where, though as publishers we recognized the intrinsic merit of the book, we underestimated its "significance" because we had not accurately evaluated the importance of the fact that it was eminently readable—"a good read"—and that, while the argument would be an important revelation to people interested in the history of Christianity and the history of social tolerance, we had no way of estimating how many people would be interested in the history of homosexuality. We took the benefit of this underestimation happily—or, if I dare put it this way: gaily.

Of course, it may be argued that had we known then what we know now, and had we printed a first edition of 17,000 copies rather than 2,500, the list price would have been considerably lower. But, then, we might have sold so many more copies than 17,000 in the first year we would probably be saying to ourselves that we should have printed 25,000, in which case the list price would have been even lower than that. However, having been mistaken in the original sales estimate, the unexpected income from that scholarly work helps cover the deficit from the unexpected lack of sales of a number of other scholarly works. Publishing is a form of gambling, not a science.

One of the charges to the participants in this conference was to consider changes that might be anticipated in publishers' volume of book and journal publishing and in anticipated markets and so on; but with regard to the eternal problem between the editorial evaluation of the intrinsic merit of a manuscript and the market evaluation of its sales potential, the only thing that I think is changing is that the anticipated sales are being calculated in shrinking—that is to say, more modest—

figures. A book that might have been printed in a first edition ten years ago of 2,000 copies or five years ago of 1,500 copies is more likely than not to be manufactured today in 1,000 copies. If no other change is made, then the list price must necessarily be higher than it was even a year ago.

Some changes have been attempted even when there has been resistance to them. In the course of the past half-dozen years we have undertaken three experiments for cost savings—to be passed on to the buyers in the form of lower list prices—which have been greatly objected to. The simplest and oldest form is to use photo-ready typescript—that is, to photograph a typewritten manuscript. The greatest resistance is from authors. I have seen strong men reduced to tears when their editors propose to publish their books by that method. The resistance is aesthetic. I have yet to meet a single scholar in the humanities who can alter his traditional "mind-set" of what a book is in order to find reproduction of his work by photographing a typewritten manuscript acceptable aesthetically.

A second experiment has been to issue new monographs of very limited specialization as original paperbacks. The average saving this brings about is a difference of approximately $5.00 so that the list price may be $20.00 rather than $25.00, or $25.00 rather than $30.00. I have yet to find a book buyer who is grateful. On the contrary, because the work in this form is seen as a paperback, the buyer is outraged by a figure of more than $20.00. We have not yet found it possible to give every book buyer a course in publishing economics to appreciate the difference between the paperback reprint of a previously published hardcover book and a new work published originally with a paperback binding.

A third experiment has been that of publishing what we call "text-fiche." This method was invented in order to make possible the publication of very heavily illustrated works, so that anywhere from 100 to 600 or 700 images in full color would be available on fiche cards along with a text in printed form. The saving to the buyer is spectacular. Instead of buying 600 slides at a dollar apiece for $600, such a text-fiche edition might sell for $100. Heavily illustrated works in archaeology, anthropology, and social history have been treated in this way as well as the ideally appropriate archives of paintings and other graphic works. The drawback to this advantage is that the images cannot be seen by the naked eye. They must be illuminated, enlarged, and projected onto a screen by a mechanical reader. Libraries have bought, installed, and made available to scholars such equipment in institutional settings. But the publisher's dream that the experiment would catch on widely enough for individual researchers to buy such readers for their own desks has been frustrated. There is no space on the desk now occupied by a word processor.

Well, it was Robert Maynard Hutchins who said that the university is charged with the necessity continually to experiment; but it would be very foolish indeed to expect that every experiment will succeed.

It is my contention that the idea of the "intrinsic value" of a scholarly manuscript is a misleading if not to say unfeasible concept. It is "academic" in the sense that gives "academic" a bad name, meaning of no practical value, that is, of the order of a purely intellectual exercise. But academics are given to intellectual exercises and this game is characterized by the attempt to estimate the value of a manuscript that could be a book under the condition of imagining its value in spite of its not being a book. It is an attempt to evaluate a contribution to scholarship in the form of a written argument without consideration of the cost of paper, printing, and binding, of composition, warehousing, marketing, postage, and so on. It is the attempt to estimate the message without the medium. But it is the medium that costs money.

The market value of the book or journal must be formulated in terms of how many people will pay how much for the message.

The grim predictions I hear are that there will be fewer graduate students and fewer faculty positions open in the future in the humanities and in the social sciences, whereas those have been traditionally the fields of heaviest concentration for publications of university presses. If there are fewer people who can afford or who will feel that they need "new knowledge and significant thought" in these disciplines, then either university presses will bring out fewer copies of them in their first printings and therefore the prices will be even higher, or they will not bring them out at all.

The prediction that is also only a rumor is that many if not all university presses are cutting back on the number of books they publish per year; this reflects the economic constraints under which they operate. Of the seventy-seven members of the Association of American University Presses it is known that more than half are operated in the red, and their deficits are covered by the operating funds of their parent universities. It is rumored that many of those universities are putting pressure on the administrators of their presses to cut those losses, to minimize those deficits, which must result in a cutback in the quantity of scholarly output.

We do not operate in a vacuum. We operate in the real world, and, while it is a real world in which academic questions are of paramount interest, economic questions come more and more to the forefront. It is not only a question of financial matters; economic questions refer in general to the best use of resources, human, material, and financial.

Thus it becomes a matter of the moral as well as the intellectual choices of our society, because choices have to be made. We cannot do everything that is desirable. Between any two goods the question is, then, which is the better of the two, and what purpose each satisfies. How these choices are made will affect the future quality of our culture.

REFERENCES

1. Boswell, John. *Christianity, Social Tolerance, and Homosexuality: Gay People in Western Europe from the Beginning of the Christian Era to the Fourteenth Century.* Chicago: University of Chicago Press, 1980.
2. Robinson, Paul. "Gay Was Beautiful." *New York Times Book Review* (August 10, 1980), pp. 12–13.

LIBRARIANS, PUBLISHERS, AND SCHOLARS, COMMON INTERESTS, DIFFERENT VIEWS: THE VIEW OF AN INDEPENDENT SCHOLARLY PUBLISHER[1]

Frederick A. Praeger[2]

Librarians, publishers, and scholars are natural partners in the creation and dissemination of knowledge. The independent scholarly publisher specializes in activities of selection, editing, and marketing in areas where the scholarly community needs fast, flexible, and enterprising support; highly specialized marketing; and a great variety of methods to produce scholarly materials in very small editions. Selecting, editing, designing, proofreading, printing, binding, and marketing are essential steps in fulfilling this role. None of these steps can be skipped and all are expensive. Scholars need access to published materials in all their variety and the traditional role of the library has been to expand their access by purchasing published materials and organizing them for appropriate retrieval. Current events have disrupted this symbiotic relationship of scholars, publishers, and libraries. New technology makes it possible for scholars to gain distribution of their works while bypassing publishers. Libraries, confronted with rising costs and relatively decreasing revenue, have turned to networks and electronic delivery systems that often save time over the imperfect working of the market. These events threaten to disrupt publishing with its unique values and endanger the life of the book, which has served us in ways that can hardly be duplicated. To deal constructively with the challenge, scholars, publishers, and librarians need to cultivate a consciousness of our dependence on each other. A national commission to study the problems and strong lobbying efforts to increase national and state support for university and public libraries and for scholarly publication are suggested.

Once upon a time, the librarian, the scholar, the publisher, and the printer were members of a community that functioned smoothly and in time-honored ways to create, to preserve, and to disseminate knowledge. While the members of this community still function much as they tradi-

1. I am grateful to Beatrice Ferrigno-Lee and Barbara Ellington of Westview Press and to Mary Biggs of the University of Chicago Graduate Library School for their editorial help, their insistence on completeness, and their many thoughtful suggestions.
2. Westview Press, 5500 Central Avenue, Boulder, Colorado 80301.

tionally have, the rapidly evolving electronic age and very serious financial constraints tend to blur the once clear distinctions and relationships among them: we live, to use Peter Drucker's phrase, in an age of discontinuity [1]. Publishers with data banks are becoming librarians; scholars with word processors and printing devices are becoming printers and publishers, and so are librarians. The collapse of the traditional distinctions is generated by electronic technology, equally available to all persons and institutions involved in information creation, storage, and transfer. The new technology and its evolution at ever-increasing speed destabilize the traditional information and knowledge community and present all of us with both problems and opportunities. How we deal with them, how creatively our community responds to this challenge, or crisis, will determine the shape of all our functions in years to come. Can we carry on with the basic business of communication in an essentially cooperative way? Are we going to fight among ourselves for privileges and market shares? Are some of us going to form alliances with small or large purveyors of the new electronic marvels? Will some of us drown in the powerful waves created by the new communication systems?

There is a lot of hopeful talk about electronic publishing, which would make information available not only in the form of books but also on chips, tapes, discs, or other machine-readable media; one could then instantly transfer the information from the publisher or data bank to, for instance, the central library of a developing country in east Africa, by simply and swiftly pressing a few buttons. Digital information traveling electronically can be read on a screen but can also be printed instantly and be assembled into something resembling a book. In either case pages could be moved or scrolled backward and forward, providing instant and random access to information and knowledge. From the standpoint of the scholar who needs access to a great variety of informational sources in order to create knowledge and who then is anxious rapidly to disseminate that knowledge, these advances may be enticing, especially if the scholar does not question the drawbacks and weaknesses of this conundrum of sources and information transfer systems. But as we analyze this complex thoughtfully we will see that it has, like so many things in life, both good and bad qualities. For many of us the negative aspects may outweigh the positive ones, for example, books and publishers are gradually becoming endangered species.

The scholar needs information and knowledge, often different kinds of knowledge—conclusions, guesses, insights, scenarios, creative interpretations, models, analogies, summaries, speculations, and the whole array of unconventional experimental thought processes and results of thought processes, the links in the chain of understanding—and, finally, more knowledge, and also wisdom. How is he going to do his job if book and publisher, the traditional depositories and transfer agents of knowledge, are eliminated from the chain? Who will do the necessary job of valuing, vetting, screening, organizing, and structuring knowledge? Who will support the dynamics, the compulsiveness, the addiction to excellence necessary to provide the service the scholarly community requires and deserves? Who will even do the indexing that helps the scholar work his way through piles of "relevant" material to find those items or thoughts that are valid, useful, and represent the accomplishment of other scholars who have worked before him or even contemporaneously?

The publisher's essential contribution to the creation of knowledge is even more important today than in the recent past. Knowledge is pushing with ever-increasing vigor into the frontiers of the knowable. We recognize that everything is part of a larger system and the larger systems are subsystems of megaconfigurations. The dynamic growth of knowledge occurs in a very unstable world in which, despite the unprecedented increase in knowledge and understanding, we are still unable to solve relatively simple problems like peace in the Middle East or the survival of the industrial base of the great Western nations. In our search for solutions we often become enchanted by magical, diaphanous illusions, such as the beneficial future of a service economy based on computers and robots.

A brief examination of the traditional functions of our community and the changes in its operational modes finds the scholar still in place as both the creator and consumer of knowledge. Previously the scholar wrote a work, turned it over to a publisher who evaluated it, sometimes accepted it, and then had it edited, typeset, proofread, printed, bound, and distributed. It easily reached libraries and individuals and perhaps contributed to yet another work that entered the same cycle. Today, the scholar in an electronically sophisticated environment can write, revise, store, and duplicate his or her work, effectively evading publisher, printer, and library. Scholars do not always do so, but alternative means of reaching an audience are certainly available.

The modern librarian, equipped with electronic data storage, access and retrieval devices, and furthermore with copiers, no longer needs to purchase single or multiple copies of a great variety of books in order to satisfy multiple demands, including books for "reserve shelves" supporting academic curricula. One copy of a book can now be made visually, or physically, accessible to many users in many places. This process still relies on the publisher, but far less than previously when libraries had to purchase many copies of works for which a high demand was anticipated or single copies to maintain comprehensive and up-to-date collections. While the use of copiers to duplicate copyrighted material is frowned on by librarians, many are forced by financial constraints and enormous pressures from faculty and students to stretch the fair use doctrine to permit users to duplicate books libraries would have purchased in the past when book budgets were larger and prices were relatively low. Many individuals, especially members of academic and research communities, freely copy published material with little concern for the law or for the rights of the author and publisher. Admittedly, money is scarce, time is precious, traditional delivery systems are sluggish, and scholars often tend to be impatient. But I find that, generally, there is a pervasive assumption that knowledge and information should be freely transmitted, and a parallel resistance to paying for them, especially when payment is so easily avoided.

Of course, not all scholars engage in the practice of unauthorized copying and, of course, some librarians scrupulously adhere to the wording of the copyright law. I realize that neither scholars nor librarians can be held accountable for the transgressions of the copying mills; in fact, I sympathize with librarians and scholars who are often faced with cumbersome and lengthy ordering and supply procedures or with painful difficulties in obtaining out-of-print material. These problems bedevil the entire publishing and bookselling industry.

The modern publisher was once, and actually still is, expected to select, edit, design, typeset, proofread, print, bind, and market works of knowledge. A publisher cannot skip any of the steps and still fulfill his role. He can sometimes dispense with traditional typesetting and proofreading when an author provides a book in camera-ready format. The publisher is still—but perhaps not for much longer—the quality control center of the scholarly information and knowledge business, picking and choosing, using his limited and costly powers of judgment and reflection in a selection process that brings order to chaos, arranges information and knowledge logically, sets priorities for superior work, and eliminates undeserving projects. The publisher must then support those choices with imaginative marketing that provides the authors with access to markets, peer communities, and special constituencies and also alerts the interested audience to the forthcoming work. And the enterprising publisher's scouts also explore the frontier areas of science, stimulating and encouraging scholars to transform their thoughts and experiments into publishable manuscripts.

The process through which a book passes in a publishing house requires large amounts of attention from intelligent, talented, and highly trained individuals. They do not come cheap. Some scholarly publishers like Westview also invest heavily in electronic equipment to make editing, typesetting, proofreading, and administration more efficient. This investment reduces production and administrative costs, but the savings are not being realized because library markets are shrinking at an alarming rate; consequently, edition sizes are becoming minimal which increases the unit costs. Even if we are able to solve some difficult problems by, for example, engineering perfect interfaces or modems that make it possible to move data from word processor to machine-readable media to a clean page in an attractive typesetter's font ready for platemaker or offset press, the fates bedeviling the publishing industry will see to it that other factors (such as postal rates and interest charges) continue to contribute to rising costs.

Even so, books, like eggs, remain bargains when we consider how much intellectual nourishment they contain. We can take a colleague to a nonfrivolous dinner for the price of a hardbound book, and while we may enjoy his conversation, we will probably learn more from the book and have an easier time retrieving the information. Furthermore, the information contained in that book will probably not be cheaper if we try to get at it by electronic means. It is true that we might get it much faster, because if we want it in book form we have to buy it, which often is an inefficient, drawn-out process since only a few books are in stock in the average bookstore. We can also obtain it through an interlibrary loan system which is nice for clients but has deadly side effects for publishers. Here we come to a disease whose symptoms can be diagnosed as most threatening to the health and survival chances of the scholarly publisher. While some librarians use the interlibrary loan system mainly for out-of-print and foreign language materials, others use it with abandon, with very little discrimination, or because of dire economic necessity. The modern librarians' beautiful world of resource sharing, networking, and interlibrary loan systems, of electronic utilities, bibliographic locators, computerized bookkeeping, copiers, printers, searching and linking devices, is a paradise of tools and gadgets in which, instead of buying books, librarians can press buttons and, like booksellers, avoid the need to stock books in depth. They often need only to locate one library that has actually bought the book or journal, apply magical electronic formulae, and, at least in theory, the book or journal article will appear in a few days on the magician's shelf.

In theory and to some extent in practice, books have been physically obsolete for many years, but we cling to them not because we are trapped in tradition but because books are comfortable, user friendly, and, like the proverbial mousetrap, a better one has not been made. We can get information and knowledge very quickly by electronic means, but that electronic transfer still has to start with a book or other visually accessible form of information that can be converted to digital signals. Once we do this to a book, we have converted a warm, loving, user-friendly informant into something cold, impersonal, and inflexible. Can we take our cathode ray tube to bed? Can we write in its margins? Can we comfortably rest and reflect or flip back and forth in a pile of printouts? Electronic media and their printed offspring do not make easy reading.

Perhaps I should interpolate here something about the independent scholarly publishers, why they are needed, and how they fit into the information business. Traditionally the community of scholars needed the particular talents and services of publishers who specialized in selecting, editing, producing, and marketing scholarly works. This type of publishing developed and was refined in Germany, the cradle of modern science. As science expanded and diversified, so did scholarly publishing, and the great German companies prospered. In the course of time scientific and scholarly publishers became important also in other European countries and eventually in the United States. The explosive, almost revolutionary, expansion of American scholarly publishing is directly connected with the migration of thousands of great European scholars to the United States before and during the Second World War. This migration included a number of experienced scholarly publishers, mostly Germans like Eric Proskauer and Walter Johnson, or Dutch like Maurits Dekker.

In the spring of 1950 Maurits Dekker gave me a two-hour lecture on the principles of scholarly publishing that convinced me I should put all my eggs into that particular basket. "It's all very simple," he said. "You never make much money and you have to accept that. You have to become a servant of science in the disciplines you choose. You must do important books even if you lose money because that will further your reputation. You must make service your number one priority and you must be willing to work eighty hours instead of the customary forty." He also admonished me to think about this profession night and day, weekdays and weekends, and added that a compulsive drive and a bit of madness were positive rather than negative qualities for this work.

My actual motives for establishing two scholarly presses in the United States and spending six years running a fairly scholarly operation in Munich were somewhat more prosaic: I had to make a living. I tried to combine what Maurits Dekker taught me with the facts that I was (and still am) a frustrated teacher, a frustrated writer, and a not so frustrated poker player—with some background in social sciences—and there you have a publisher.

Dekker gave me a copy of the *British Bookseller,* the London equivalent of our *Publishers Weekly,* which offered several titles for which I perceived an American market. My first two choices were Hans Kelsen's *The Law of the United Nations* [2] and Hersch Lauterpacht's *International Law and Human Rights* [3]. This was the beginning of Praeger Publishers in

New York, which applied the publishing approach of Interscience and Academic Press to the social sciences and multidisciplinary areas such as international affairs, military science, and area studies. The company with which I am now connected, Westview Press, is an intellectual successor, but not an exact copy, of the old Praeger company, which still exists as a division of CBS Educational and Scientific Publishing.

I have been asked why such firms are needed, what is their utility, their function, in a publishing world that has many great university presses, and large specialized operations (such as McGraw-Hill, Wiley, and Prentice-Hall) and where many scholarly books are published by trade houses such as Harper and Row's Basic Books, and Norton. Westview sometimes competes with university presses and with some of the trade publishers who issue important nonfiction books, but that is not where we make our most valuable contribution. We function best in the areas where the scholarly community needs specialized, fast, flexible, and enterprising support, where it needs intimacy and sympathy, highly specialized marketing, and a great variety of ways to produce scholarly materials in very small editions. Scholars and libraries need publishers like Westview because, as a group, we are somewhat less conventional, more flexible, and faster than most of our competitors. We can break even with very small editions. We give great scope to our editors, who are encouraged to be intimately involved with and supportive of our authors. We are fundamentally service oriented and have devised a creative system that combines a knowledge-factory approach with some elements of a Tiffany-quality operation. We try to be modest and frugal, maintaining a low overhead so we can publish upper-level texts in small editions which reflect innovation, originality, and the frontier spirit that typifies the leading edge of research.

Today the independent scholarly publisher (let us not use the term "commercial" publisher), who has no access to the support systems usually provided to university presses, is in a difficult position. While the publisher still services authors and libraries, authors and libraries need the publisher less and less. While publishers and authors still feel that scholarly information should be properly edited and printed, the economic realities demand that publishers be less selective, provide less editing, and produce less durable and more inexpensive books. Economic realities lead them further and further from the traditional role of selector and purveyor of information, to a position more like that of a printer, who simply duplicates what is submitted to him.

This unfortunate trend is encouraged by the shrinking library market: the unwillingness or inability of the library community to provide the market the publisher needs leads to the vicious circle of smaller print runs and larger unit costs, lower editorial and production standards, less latitude for risk taking, no funding for reprints, leaving thousands of our best books unobtainable, which seriously hampers research, and so on. If scholarly publishers cannot sell enough books even with generous promotion budgets and comprehensive distribution systems, how can they afford the dedicated professionals needed to select, edit, produce, and market books?

What is needed at this juncture is more gatherings like this one. I frequently speak with librarians who are aware of the plight of publishers, but many of them continue to focus exclusively on the consumer, on providing rapid access to information already available. They often disregard the need for the publishers' efforts to organize and market information, and they often tend to ignore the cost of that process. Working with inadequate budgets, they sometimes do not consider the authors' need to get their work into the marketplace, into the exchange system of idea and thought. This lack of awareness or sensitivity often stifles dialogue and makes it difficult for the publisher to adjust to the realities of the future. Perhaps the publisher's role needs to be redefined, perhaps we all need to adjust to a technological world that is moving too fast for our comfort, but I would like to see us arriving at new definitions in concert rather than each in our own semi-isolated discipline. The path by which knowledge is conveyed from author to publisher to library and scholar is becoming constricted and crisscrossed with shortcuts on which we are all moving at different paces, but we must still go forward together in some sort of rough synchronization. We need a philosophy, perhaps an informal policy, and we need the consciousness of mutual dependence so that we can not only deal constructively with the challenge but also intelligently take advantage of our opportunities.

I have no pat solutions to offer, but I would like to make a few recommendations:

1. We need to understand better the problems of our partners. I have myself worked in a library, have taught librarians, and have made it a habit to consult with them during most of my long publishing life. I understand and appreciate librarians' problems and certainly understand the librarians' mission. But many of my colleagues do not, so there needs to be a much greater educational exchange. Librarians in turn need to understand that the publisher functions as a link in the communication chain—if that link is broken, the system will fail or, as our computer people would say, crash.

2. I think we need a high-powered commission, perhaps on a national level, supported by a major research effort and perhaps financed by an organization such as the Annenberg Foundation. It would define problems, identify trends, and develop a team approach to bridge gaps that

at present seem to become wider as new information technologies mature. We also need a much better—that means implacable, fierce, unrelenting—lobbying effort at both national (we do have many powerful friends in Congress) and state levels to press for funds for university and public libraries as well as for scholarly publication grants for those university presses and independent publishers whose primary function is service to the scholarly community. Researchers and research institutions must also be able to obtain grants that include support for publication of their work. At this time most grants fund research only—but of what value is research that does not reach the intended audience?

To summarize: we must understand each other better and cooperatively promote our concerns. We cannot permit the book to drown in electronic tidal waves; we must maintain it as the central, indispensable instrument of scholarship and scientific progress and relate it creatively to the incremental growth of electronic technology.

REFERENCES

1. Drucker, Peter F. *The Age of Discontinuity: Guidelines to Our Changing Society.* New York: Harper & Row, 1969.
2. Kelsen, Hans. *The Law of the United Nations: A Critical Analysis of Its Fundamental Problems.* New York: F. A. Praeger, 1950.
3. Lauterpacht, Hersch. *International Law and Human Rights.* New York: F. A. Praeger, 1950.

THE VIEW OF A FOR-PROFIT SCIENTIFIC PUBLISHER

Peter F. Urbach[1]

Increased publishing costs and decreasing library budgets are chief among the interrelated problems that confront libraries and publishers. Librarians seek to solve their financial crises by resource sharing, networking, photocopying, and more selective acquisition. Publishers seek to solve their financial problems by publishing more selectively, automating production operations, increasing prices, and developing new distribution channels to reach new markets. Some of these "solutions" pit librarians and publishers against each other. There is no easy, short-term resolution of these conflicts. We are now on the threshold of major technological change which will radically alter the way in which information is disseminated. Online systems, new document distribution systems, and new information access mechanisms will alter the basic relationships among authors, publishers, librarians, and users. It is these changes that will provide the solutions to the present conflicts.

I speak from the perspective of a scientific and technical publisher, in the for-profit sector, moving rapidly into the use of the new technologies. Pergamon is a large traditional scientific and technical publisher that goes beyond just publishing. Pergamon has operated its own printing establishments in Europe for a number of years, printing many of its books and journals. Several years ago, Pergamon acquired a controlling interest in a company then known as the British Printing Corporation, the largest printing company in Europe, with about forty plants. The British Printing and Communication Corporation (BPCC), as it is now known, prints packages, labels, and record album covers as well as books, magazines, and the Sunday supplements to newspapers. The printing conglomerate BPCC has a larger sales volume than its parent, Pergamon Press. Coser has alluded to the phenomenon of the large nonpublishing conglomerate that buys a publishing house only to find that it does not know the business [1]. In Pergamon we have the publish-

1. Pergamon International Information Corporation, 1340 Old Chain Bridge Road, McLean, Virginia 22101.

ing house that bought the conglomerate, and the chief executive of the conglomerate is, in fact, a scientific publisher.

My orientation is not that of the traditional scientific publisher but rather that of the new electronic publisher. As such, it is different from that of the preceding contributors to this issue and that may explain why my conclusions with respect to the subject of this conference are also different.

During this conference we have been discussing a single very depressing theme which has been repeated by each of the preceding authors. Libraries are the major customers for the product of the scholarly and technical publisher. Library budgets are down. As a result, book sales are down. Publishers' costs go up, and therefore, with sales down and costs up, publishers raise prices. Sales continue to go down and prices continue to go up. Publishers cut the number of book titles they publish and are more selective in what they choose to publish. These are not textbooks that sell tens of thousands of copies but fairly narrow-interest technical works where a relatively small loss of sales can make the difference between profit and loss. Journals do a bit better than the books, but the problem is the same and the advent of extensive library resource sharing and photocopying cuts deeply into the journal business.

What does all this leave for the for-profit publisher? Book sales are down and journals are surviving but losing ground. We have turned aggressively to electronic publishing, and we believe the solutions to the problems lie with the new technology.

Research libraries and the scientific and technical publishers have always worked closely together, each playing a unique and important role in making information available to the user community. The relationship between the two has not, however, been without its difficulties. The advent of modern photocopying, library networking, resource sharing, increased production costs and increasing prices in the face of decreasing library budgets are some of the interrelated issues that confront libraries and publishers.

Libraries seek to solve their financial crisis by resource sharing, networking, photocopying, more selective acquisition, and sometimes user charges. Publishers seek to solve their financial problems by publishing more selectively, automating production operations, increasing prices, and developing new distribution channels to reach new markets.

Some of these "solutions" to the problem simply pit libraries and publishers more intensively against each other. Libraries will continue to buy less and share more in order to get the best value for their shrinking dollar. Publishers will continue to produce products that their customers urgently require and for which they can charge prices that will permit them to remain profitable in spite of shrinking markets. There is no easy resolution of these conflicts.

There have been many studies to attempt to quantify these factors: how much photocopying? how much resource sharing? how much have subscriptions declined? how much have costs gone up? how much have prices gone up? The specific numbers are arguable but the trends are clear: libraries and publishers are both caught in a squeeze that may be a two-person zero-sum game; one side wins only when the other side loses. If that is in fact the situation, how can a dialogue between librarians and publishers such as called for by this conference help? Does a dialogue between opposing chess players lead to the resolution of the conflict on the board? Libraries and publishers are locked in a symbiotic relationship to make the publisher's product available to the library user. Neither can fulfill the task without the other. A continuing dialogue is certainly desirable to ensure that the joint task of creating and distributing information is done effectively, but if each can only gain at the expense of the other, what can a dialogue truly achieve? In my view, the future of these difficult issues will be resolved not by further dialogue between the parties but by advances in the technology.

We are now on the threshold of major technological change which will radically alter the way in which information is disseminated. It will also alter the basic relationship between authors, publishers, librarians, and users. It is these changes that will provide the solutions and also develop new relationships among the players. We are still trying to adjust to the ubiquitous photocopy machine, which already seems to have always been with us. We are also trying to adjust to regional and national library networks, instant communication for interlibrary loan, vast electronic bibliographic databases, and some electronic full-text retrieval and electronic typesetting systems. We are also witnessing the proliferation of the microcomputer, which is leading to yet another generation of change, the introduction of lower-cost, higher-speed facsimile devices and lower-cost, broad-band telecommunications. Can there possibly be more that we have to confront? I believe "we ain't seen nothin' yet."

In addition to the changes brought about by the cost-price-budget squeeze, the proliferation of photocopying and the automation of interlibrary loan, the relationship between publishers and libraries is changing dramatically with the rapid growth of online computer services provided by the nonpublisher vendors. It is true, as the critics of the new technology say, that you cannot take a cathode ray tube (CRT) to bed, but neither can you take the many bound volumes of the case law of the state of Illinois or the hard copy of the Chemical Abstract Service to bed. Both of these subjects are searched far better on CRTs connected to an online database than in the traditional printed products.

The online services have gone well beyond full text of law and secondary bibliographic scientific information. They are now in all fields, and full-text services are beginning to proliferate. With these services, the product is radically different not just in form and technology but also in terms of how it is used and how it is priced. The online vendor sells access to information or computer time or output, not books, not journals, not even journal articles. This difference will have a profound effect on users, libraries, authors, publishers, and online vendors.

It is now the computer vendor who provides access to information to the library and the library's customers, not the publisher. This is not the same as having the present distributor or a subscription agent interposed between the publisher and the librarian to act as facilitator, making the publisher's wares easily available to the library. The library is not the publisher's customer, but the customer of the online vendor. The library pays the online vendor on the basis of actual use and the online vendor in turn pays a royalty to the publisher.

The relationships between the publisher, the online vendor, and the library customer are governed by explicit contractual agreements among the parties. Here there is no opportunity for fair-use photocopying, resource sharing, or networking, except to the extent that the parties contractually agree. The publisher–online vendor contract often precludes the publisher's gaining access to the identities of the customers or having any influence on the pricing of the product or even the form in which the product is made available to the user. Is it possible that these relationships that we see emerging in these still early days of online services will set the pattern for the future relationships between publishers and libraries? Are today's online services with their bibliographic or full-text legal databases the model for the relationships between publishers and libraries with full-text electronic books and journals in the future?

Some publishers looking at how these relationships are evolving are not content to let the online vendors interpose themselves between the publishers and their customers. Just as some publishers choose not to contract out their typesetting, printing, and distribution but prefer to do it themselves, some publishers are now choosing to integrate their operations and serve as their own online vendors. Pergamon is such a publisher. We have our own typesetting and printing companies to produce our books and journals. Similarly, and for similar reasons, we have acquired our own online service, Pergamon InfoLine, a computer-based online service located in London, which provides electronic access to a growing number of Pergamon publications.

Other publishers are following a similar strategy. The Chemical Abstracts Service and the Institute for Scientific Information have both recently moved into the distribution of their electronic products themselves. The publishers and libraries do not have a monopoly on troublesome relationships. Publishers and online vendors have also been known to disagree on priorities, on quality control, and on how the limited revenue pie is to be sliced. The publisher often feels a need for or actually requires control of the computer environment and distribution of the information directly to the end user for both technical and business reasons. Other publishers, however, continue to choose external online vendors, but as the information transmitted electronically becomes more complex, involving special scientific notation, mathematics, chemistry, and graphics, the general purpose online vendor who is geared to handle straight text may not be able to meet the publishers' requirements for special software and hardware.

In either case, the electronic distribution of information from the publisher's database via the online computer to libraries and end users, with charges based on use or on the amount of information provided, will eliminate some of the current issues between libraries and publishers. Fair-use photocopying, resource sharing, and networking will no longer be issues. A whole new spectrum of issues will, of course, be raised, with a whole new terminology. For example, we now have the "downloading issue" and the problem of users shifting to higher speed terminals to reduce access time and thereby cut their costs. The new technology may also have a profound impact on what is published in the future. If revenue is not based on purchase but on actual use, journal articles that are not read will contribute little to the publisher's revenue. Won't this have an interesting impact on how the publisher operates?

Although we are witnessing rapid change in technology, we cannot expect to jump quickly from today's technology and today's habits to the fully electronic journal where the end user gets the information solely from the CRT screen. Initially, the centralized electronic databases may be used to produce paper copy facsimiles of the original journal pages for the user at remote locations. These remote on-demand printing systems will link the publisher's database to the research library or the industrial center. The user will have rapid access to current information without present-day distribution delays. The library may well pay for the service on a per-page or per-article basis, possibly in combination with a more traditional subscription fee.

We already find publishers moving into on-demand document distribution, using both conventional technology and new forms of product distribution. As one example, Pergamon has recently developed an association with Information on Demand (IOD), a Berkeley, California, information broker which provides rapid delivery of journal articles on demand. A number of libraries use this service, often in preference to the conventional and less rapid interlibrary loan, but it is used principally by special libraries which have an urgent need for material they cannot quickly acquire. There is little high technology involved, just electronic order transmission from IOD to its order fulfillment people; photocopying is the basic technology involved. The service differs from interlibrary loan in one significant respect: IOD pays copyright royalties on every copy made.

Another example: John Wiley now offers its books and journals as an on-demand supplier over the Dialog DialOrder system. The customer can place the order for the Wiley book directly on the terminal. The Dialog computer transmits the order to Wiley, which then fills the order. Each end user or library orders directly from the publisher through the online vendor's computer. This is yet another new form of distribution relationship between the publisher and the customer. We can expect additional publishers to move to offer similar document delivery services to insure that they remain in the business of distributing the documents they publish.

A consortium of major scientific and technical publishers recently undertook an intensive market research effort to evaluate optical disc technology to handle single-copy document distribution of journal articles. Known as the ADONIS project, the intensive study effort has not yet led to an operational system, but the amount of effort that went into it indicates the seriousness with which publishers view their entry into on-demand document delivery services.

I have no doubt that something like ADONIS will be implemented in the near future. The evolution of these services might involve research libraries as suppliers, customers, or competitors of publishers. The use of the new technologies in document delivery will require centralization of large document collections, which is probably likely to lead to partnerships among publishers and between publishers and libraries.

Libraries today must deal with the urgent need to share resources and to cut collections to stretch declining library budgets while continuing to serve their users' needs. Publishers today must deal with declining revenues stemming from the very solutions that the libraries adopt to solve their problems. There is a clear need for serious library-publisher dialogue, as the conference theme suggests, but can publishers really expect libraries to turn away from their elegant electronic interlibrary loan systems and once again begin to purchase multiple copies? Or can libraries reasonably expect publishers not to react adversely to the new systems being introduced by the libraries, which cut the publishers' income? The conflicts are not likely to be resolved, but they are likely to be of limited duration and will ultimately be won not by one party or the other but by changes in the technology which will, we can hope, permit both parties to win together.

REFERENCE

1. Coser, Lewis A. "The Publishing Industry as a Hybrid." In this issue.

THE PROFESSIONAL SOCIETY IN A CHANGING WORLD

Rita G. Lerner[1]

The goals of a professional society as publisher differ from those of the commercial publisher, since the society exists for the purpose of serving its members. Examples are given of the types of activities which a society engages in, and publishing expenses are shown as a large component of society programs. Computer composition of journals and cooperation between primary and secondary services will help to hold down the escalating costs of publishing. New technology also offers new ways to store and distribute information.

It is characteristic of the scientific and technical periodical industry in the United States that there is a wide variety of types of publisher. It has been estimated that, in 1977, 38 percent of the scientific and technical journals in the United States were published by societies and associations, 29 percent by commercial publishers, 14 percent by educational institutions, and 19 percent by other organizations [1, p. 90]. According to a report by the Royal Society, about 65 percent of the 1,500 journals in the natural sciences in the United Kingdom are produced by learned societies, associations, and institutions [2, p. 28]. The same British study noted that, before World War II, the publication of scientific journals was largely the preserve of the learned societies; however, since 1945 several multinational companies, such as Pergamon Press and Elsevier–North Holland, have established large journal publishing operations which have grown rapidly [2, p. 28].

The purpose of any professional society is the advancement and diffusion of knowledge in that discipline. In the United States, a professional society usually enjoys the status of a tax-exempt educational institution, which confers certain benefits as well as certain responsibilities. There are responsibilities to the discipline and other responsibilities to the general public.

1. American Institute of Physics, 335 East 45th Street, New York, New York 10017.

The management of any publishing operation has the same high hopes for a good-quality product, whether the publisher is a commercial organization or a society. A commercial publishing house has a clear-cut directive from its board of directors to operate a growing and profitable, or at any rate not unprofitable, business. A society, however, has a board of directors consisting of members of the profession, and their interests lie in advancing the discipline. Through the board and advisory committees, the members of the society are deeply involved in setting publishing policy. The members are simultaneously the authors, the editors, the referees, the subscribers, and the readers. Members are the backbone of any society publishing program, functioning also as the initiators of new journals and the arbiters of the success or failure of journals [3]. As authors, they want the widest possible circulation of their papers in a prestigious journal. A survey by the British Institute of Physics [4] studied how physics authors selected the journals they published in. In rank order, the first five criteria were: circulation size, speed of publication, reputation of the publisher, refereeing, and quality of production. The editors, who usually receive an honorarium which does not represent the true value of their time, also want a broad circulation and a physically attractive final product. The referees are volunteers, who are frequently chosen because they publish in a particular journal; their reward comes in knowing that they have contributed to maintaining the quality and integrity of the journal—and quality frequently (but not always) goes hand in hand with circulation. The members are subscribers either directly, as a benefit of membership, or indirectly through recommendations to libraries. As subscribers and readers, they expect the lowest possible cost of acquisition. As members of a profession, they also require a variety of services unrelated to publishing.

Another major difference between commercial and society publishers is in the area of growth and capital investment. A society usually has no risk capital for new ventures and is frequently hard put to find money for research, development, and investment in new equipment to replace that outmoded by advancing technology. Another difference between society and commercial publishers, according to the Royal Society report, is that learned societies tend to create new journals by dividing journals of broad scope into several more specialized ones; commercial publishers are more active in seeking wholly new journals, either by starting them or by publishing journals for the smaller societies.

The American Institute of Physics (AIP) provides a good example of society operations. The institute is actually a membership corporation of nine member societies, for whom the institute provides an editorial processing center, central accounting and dues collections, and other services such as arranging meetings and exhibits as requested. For itself and its member societies, AIP publishes and distributes a total of 24 archival journals and 20 translation journals, as well as conference proceedings, directories, bulletins, a monthly magazine, an abstracts journal, a computer database, and various reference books and special projects. Six of the archival journals and 18 of the translation journals belong directly to the institute; the others are published by the institute for the member societies. A total of over 100,000 pages is published per year, which makes the institute the largest journal publisher in a single discipline in the world. In addition, AIP acts as the North American representative for the journals of the Institute of Physics (U.K.), and for publications of the Fachinformationszentrum Energie Physik Mathematik in Germany and the Israel Physical Society.

Table 1 shows an approximate breakdown of AIP's 1982 budget by category. Publishing operations account for over three-quarters of the operating expenses and almost all of the income which is needed to support educational services. Other operations include financial services, such as the collection of dues for member societies, subscription fulfillment for the foreign societies, and special projects.

The category "educational services" includes the programs shown in table 2. The Public Information Division sends out news releases and holds press conferences to announce important developments in physics and astronomy. It also prepares a year-end summary of the events of the year for science writers and teachers and holds educational seminars for science writers. The division produces several records annually for radio

TABLE 1
1982 EXPENSES ($)

Publishing operations	20,772,000
Educational services	1,675,000
Other operations	4,841,000

TABLE 2
EDUCATIONAL SERVICES ACTIVITIES ($)

Public information	414,000
Physics history	300,000
Manpower statistics	351,000
Society of Physics students	242,000
Graduate programs, books	134,000
Directory of physics and astronomy staff members	88,000
Manpower placement	146,000
Total	1,675,000

stations; each record has a number of two-minute spots popularizing some aspect of physics. In addition, videocassettes are prepared which go to hundreds of television stations. Each cassette contains five two-minute stories on subjects such as the physics of sports, astrophysics, medical physics, and forensics.

The Physics History Division maintains archives and photographs, conducts oral history studies, advises laboratories on setting up archives, and operates the Niels Bohr Library. The Manpower Statistics Division conducts studies on trends in undergraduate and graduate studies as well as on career trends.

Publishing is the largest component of any society's programs. To offer some insight into the costs associated with publishing journals, table 3 gives the 1982 figures associated with the 6 archival journals published directly by AIP (*Applied Physics Letters, Journal of Applied Physics, Journal of Chemical Physics, Journal of Mathematical Physics, Physics of Fluids,* and *Review of Scientific Instruments*), which constitute a yearly total of 36,000 pages. The miscellaneous category includes journals on microfilm and microfiche, storage, insurance, back numbers, and so forth. The income for these 6 journals comes from a variety of sources, as shown in table 4.

The largest source of income is subscriptions, with nonmember subscriptions accounting for two-thirds of the total number, and more than three-quarters of subscription income. The voluntary page charge, which was instituted by AIP over fifty years ago, is in effect a subsidy of the prepublication costs by the authors or their institutions [5]. The page charges are not requested until after a paper has been accepted for publication, and a paper will be published whether or not the charge is paid. Each journal has a page budget for the year which determines how

TABLE 3
1982 JOURNAL EXPENSES

	Amount	%
Editorial	1,360,000	27
Composition	1,378,000	28
Illustrations	50,000	1
Paper	525,000	10
Printing and binding	506,000	10
Mailing	468,000	9
Subscription fulfillment	142,000	3
Reprints	362,000	7
Miscellaneous	235,000	5
Total	5,026,000	

TABLE 4
1982 JOURNAL INCOME

	Amount	%
Voluntary page charges	2,039,000	33
Subscriptions	3,835,000	61
Advertising	57,000	1
Microfilm sales	67,000	1
Back number sales	29,000	1
Reprint sales	141,000	2
Royalties	32,000	1
Total	6,200,000	

many pages can be published without a page charge; this means, in practical terms, that publication of the so-called non-honoreds may have to be delayed if too many non-honoreds come in to a particular journal. Despite inflation, publication page charges at AIP today are only about 20 percent higher than they were in 1970; this is due mainly to the use of new technology to contain the rising costs of editorial management, editorial mechanics, composition, and illustrations. Approximately half of all articles published in the United States today are subsidized by page charges, submission fees, reprint fees, or some other form of fee [1, p. 74]. AIP has been fortunate in that authors appearing in its publications have a relatively high rate of honoring these page charges; this has been a major factor enabling AIP and its member societies to keep subscription prices relatively low in comparison with those of commercial journals and the European journals, many of which do not have a page charge system. Although page charges have not been customary in England, the Royal Society report suggested them as a means of keeping British journal costs low. How many authors pay page charges? In the case of AIP journals, about 85 percent do. According to a study by King and Roderer [6, p. 47], the average page charge collection for all U.S. physics journals was 89 percent, and for all science journals 33 percent. The British Institute of Physics study showed that, worldwide, physicists ranked page charges as a more important consideration in deciding where to publish than did American physicists, who gave page charges the lowest importance [7, p. 121]. Table 5 shows the 1982 subscription price per page, or per thousand words, for a sample of journals published by AIP.

Since editorial and composition costs are fixed, regardless of number of subscribers, the journals with the largest numbers of pages and the largest circulations, such as the *Physical Review,* have the lowest subscription prices per page. The Soviet journals, which have no page charges

TABLE 5
PRICE PER PAGE (¢)

Journal of Chemical Physics	3.0
Physical Review	3.1
Journal of Applied Physics	3.6
Review of Scientific Instruments	6.7
Journal of Mathematical Physics	8.1
Soviet Physics—JETP	17.4
Soviet Physics—Acoustics	34.2

and bear the added expense of translation, cost far more per page, although the relationship of cost to number of pages and size of circulation still holds true. In constant dollars, there has been almost no change in these prices since 1970.

Since the late 1960s, most publishers have experienced a steady decline in the number of subscriptions to their printed journals. Figure 1 shows the total member and nonmember subscriptions since 1970 for the 6 AIP archival journals; over a thirteen-year period, subscriptions have declined by 28 percent. Several factors are probably responsible for this. Scientists and engineers may be relying less on personal subscriptions and more on library subscriptions, preprints, reprints, and photocopies. Libraries are canceling multiple subscriptions and are using interlibrary loan for the less frequently read journals. As subscriptions decrease, the unit cost of the remaining subscriptions will increase, since the fixed expenses will be averaged over a smaller number of subscriptions. We can expect to see a continuing increase in subscription price and a continuing decline in the number of subscriptions.

Where will all of this lead journal publishers in the future? Publishers and librarians are both operating under severe financial restraints, and

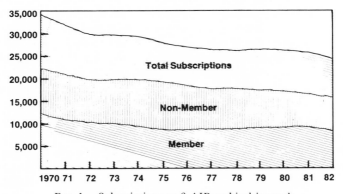

FIG. 1.—Subscriptions to 6 AIP archival journals

there are many challenges to the viability of the publication system. There are also opportunities to serve our constituencies (members and libraries) better.

For publishers, composition is the area which holds the greatest promise of containing costs and therefore subscription prices. A great deal of work has been done in the area of computer composition, which presents a special problem for scientific and technical journals. Because of the many special characters, such as Greek letters, and the requirement to set complicated mathematical equations, it is not possible to compose a journal article on the kind of word-processing equipment that is becoming so widely available. There are about half a dozen operating systems which can set the display equations used in scientific journals. One of the most popular is the UNIX system, which was developed at Bell Laboratories and has since been installed at many universities. AIP has begun to accept manuscripts from authors which have been composed on the UNIX system, although there are not yet any standards for uniformity among the UNIX users. The ATEX system, which is used by AIP and many of the larger newspapers and magazines throughout the country, also has a mathematics package which is suitable for journals.

Typically, a manuscript sent to an AIP journal editor at a remote location is logged in, either manually or by a computer which generates all the necessary correspondence. One or more referees are chosen from the reviewer file, which, for the larger journals, is computerized. If the manuscript is accepted for publication, it is sent to the institute for copy editing and keyboarding on either the ATEX or UNIX systems. The tape resulting from the keyboarding is used to drive a Videocomp device, which produces a photostat of the text. Meanwhile, the illustrations are prepared in the proper size. Text and illustrations are then pasted up to provide camera-ready copy for the printer. The abstracts are collected on tape to produce the SPIN database, which is used by various customers and online services; the tape service is current with the printed publications, since it is an outgrowth of the production process. The database is also used to create journal indexes and a printed abstract journal, *Current Physics Index.*

One obstacle to total computer photocomposition of scientific and technical material has not yet been overcome: line and halftone illustrations must be digitized. Although the technology is available and is widely used by large-circulation magazines and newspapers, the cost of illustration-scanning devices is still too high to be used economically by scientific publishers. Total computer photocomposition of scientific and technical articles will have to await developments in this area.

An important advantage of computer photocomposition, and a major reason for preferring it to other forms of composition, is that it offers the opportunity to create a database which can be reused for purposes other than journal article publication. The heads of journal articles, consisting of titles, authors, and their affiliations, abstracts, and bibliographic citations, which exist in machine-readable form, can be used to produce journal indexes, provide input to secondary services, and generate data-descriptive records, including full text, for information analysis centers. Avoiding redundant keyboarding and editing results in reduced costs for the production of information resources. Such resource sharing between primary and secondary publishers has already begun. The American Institute of Physics, for example, has been providing heads, including abstracts from its journals, on magnetic tape to the U.S. Department of Energy for input to its Energy Data Base and to the Fachinformationszentrum in Germany for the comprehensive physics abstracts journal, *Physics Briefs.*

Such resource sharing requires close cooperation among all the users. There must be agreement on the data elements to be included on the tape; even more important, standards must be specified for the content of those data elements or the result would be form without content. Efforts along these lines began in the 1970s and resulted in the publication of the UNISIST *Reference Manual for Machine-readable Descriptions* in 1974 [8] and 1981 [9]. Subsequently, meetings were held among the Association of Scientific Information Dissemination Centers (ASIDIC), the European Association of Information Centers (EUSIDIC), the National Federation of Abstracting and Information Services (NFAIS), and the International Council of Scientific Unions Abstracting Board (ICSU/AB), resulting in recommendations for the content of certain major data elements.

An impediment to interchange among primary publishers and secondary services is uncertainty about several provisions of the new U.S. Copyright Law and the variations that exist in the copyright laws of other countries. The increasing accessibility of online and batch-processing information services, together with the availability of document delivery services, has combined to create a system which could threaten the financial stability of research journals. It is the secondary services which receive the royalties on abstracts, which are frequently taken verbatim from journals; and many document delivery services do not pay royalties on copies made. This system bypasses the journal publisher and denies him both participation in the distribution of his material and recompense for his investment in his publication.

The economic impact of search services combined with document delivery services has become a matter of increasing concern to journal publishers, whether they are in the not-for-profit or the commercial sector. By sharing the input cost for abstracts, secondary services can help to ensure the continuing economic stability of their basic resource; and by paying fair royalties for copies, users and document delivery services can help ensure that publishers will have the necessary funds to meet refereeing, editorial, and production costs.

So far, the emphasis has been on the use of the computer in support of the traditional journal publication process. In practice, the decreasing costs of computer storage and communication have made it possible to consider electronic alternatives to the traditional printed journal.

King [1, 10] and others [11] have pointed out that the use of scientific and technical information tends to be highly skewed; many journal articles are infrequently used, and a small proportion of articles accounts for most use. All articles, however, are processed in the same manner. One of the important features of alternative electronic systems is that articles can be handled differently depending on their potential frequency of use. New technology for document delivery has made it possible to send copies of single articles on demand over great distances at relatively low cost, in real time. Facsimile transmitters, which range in price from $29 per month to $269 per month, can send a copy of a single page in thirty seconds to four minutes. Slow-scan cameras offer the possibility of delivering page images to a cathode ray tube at a remote location; additional equipment can provide a hard copy at the receiving end. Slow-scan cameras have the additional advantage that they can transmit from bound copies of books and journals, unlike the facsimile transmitters now on the market which can accept only single pages. The National Science Foundation has supported several experiments on document delivery. One experiment, performed at the American Institute of Physics, involved online database searching of AIP's SPIN database on DIALOG and full-text document delivery via facsimile transmitter to several National Aeronautics and Space Administration laboratories and related facilities. The study found the technology viable, but the use of the system depended a great deal on how the librarian at each laboratory site presented the service to patrons. Human factors were found to be critical to the acceptance of a new information system. Given the option, patrons chose the traditional printed product over the electronic journal [12]. There appears to be a cost on the order of five dollars per article associated with this method of delivery, exclusive of any royalty to the journal publisher. Because commercial communications facilities are changing rapidly, it is now possible for organizations to set up satellite antennas on roofs and in parking lots and make the cost of telecommunications independent of distance. (Communications satellites in the twelve-to-fourteen-gigaHertz range have antennas of only ten to fifteen feet in diameter, requiring very little space.) It is likely that the next ten years will see the widespread use of satellite communications.

The Commission of the European Communities (CEC) has been exploring the potential for using Euronet, a Europe-wide transmission network, or another telecommunications network for electronic document ordering and full-text delivery. In 1979, the CEC commissioned Arthur D. Little to study the feasibility of converting a document into digital form, storing it in a computer database, and delivering it on demand by digital communications to a user's terminal or printer. This study, known as the ARTEMIS[2] Report [13], states that such an electronic delivery system on a large scale is now technically feasible and could be more economical than conventional methods of document delivery. The report cites target delivery and printing costs, exclusive of copyright royalty, on the order of 50¢ to $1.50 per page for facsimile transmission, depending on user volume. The ARTEMIS Report concludes that market forces alone will not bring such a system into being because the scale of the operation and the extent of cooperation needed between parties with different interests are beyond what small co-ventures can achieve. The report recommends that technical trials be started. It also notes that agreement must be sought on the proper protection of intellectual property.

In yet another recent development, a consortium of commercial publishers approached the British Library Lending Division to explore possible arrangements for an electronic document delivery service, ADONIS,[3] that would be attractive to publishers and the library's users. Such an agreement would involve the creation of a machine-readable store of documents from which single articles could be produced at a low cost. Significant capital investment would be required and such a venture would be viable only if both commercial and society publishers cooperated in the system.

New forms of information storage are rapidly being developed, and their cost is decreasing. Video discs, written and read by laser beams, can store 108,000 frames on a disk, at 1,000 characters per frame. Holographic storage, which is still being developed commercially, offers the advantage of sufficient redundancy of information so that, even if a portion of the hologram should be destroyed, the remainder can still reproduce the whole; holograms on a four-by-six-inch microfiche can store as much as 2×10^8 bits of information in 20,000 holograms. One can even foresee a system which writes and reads information using ion or electron beams. It has been estimated by Richard Feynman [14] that 24 million volumes could be stored in this fashion in the surface area of 1 million pinheads or about three square yards; this would contain all of the information ever recorded by mankind in books. If an electron

2. Automatic Retrieval of Text from Europe's Multinational Information Service.
3. Article Delivery over Network Information Services.

microscope could be built with improved resolving power, it would be possible to store all the books in the world in one pinhead, or in a cube of material only 0.02 inch wide. As Feynman has pointed out, there is plenty of room at the bottom.

All of this technology can make possible a new form of archival journal. The electronic journal can be established by a group of authors with local or network access to a time-sharing computer. An author keyboards his article into a computer file and authorizes the editor to look at the file and copy it. The editor selects the referees, who are given access to the file. The referees evaluate the article, entering their suggestions and comments into the file. The author may revise his article, and the editor enters it into the journal archive, which is a public file in a computer, available to subscribers. The electronic journal has no publication deadlines and can publish new articles as soon as they are accepted by the editor.

Application of these new technologies can bestow many benefits. Among these are improvement in the linkages between primary and secondary services and between primary journals and the centers that evaluate and distribute numerical data. New linkages will require the development of standards for interfacing the components of the information transfer system. The electronic journal can lead to a decrease in publication delays and act as a means of holding down production costs in publishing. Certain conflicts of interest involving the rights of the authors, the publishers, the libraries, and the readers must still be resolved before electronic publishing can be fully realized.

One other area where change is imminent is in the publication of highly specialized books with short print runs. A new Internal Revenue Service tax ruling in the Thor Power Tool case makes it uneconomical for a commercial organization to maintain unsold inventories for any length of time. With this change in the tax situation we can expect that commercial publishers will print fewer issues of a monograph or text, will not reprint, and may even destroy remaining volumes.

I have outlined some of the challenges and opportunities which we face together as librarians and publishers: budget constraints, the costs of journal publishing, and some new technologies which are applicable to publishing. We shall sink or swim together, and I hope there will be a buoyant response.

REFERENCES

1. King, Donald W.; McDonald, Dennis D.; and Roderer, Nancy K. *Scientific Journals in the United States.* Stroudsburg, Pa.: Hutchinson Ross Publishing Co., 1981.
2. The Royal Society. *A Study of the Scientific Information System in the United Kingdom.* British Library R&D Report no. 5626. London: Royal Society, May 1981.

3. Bowen, D. H. Michael. "Member Subscriptions." In *Economics of Scientific Journals*, edited by the Ad Hoc Committee on Economics of Publication. Bethesda, Md.: Council of Biology Editors, Inc., 1982.
4. Institute of Physics. *Author/Subscriber Survey*. Bristol: Institute of Physics, 1976.
5. Marks, Robert H. "Journal Income: A Multipublisher's View." In *Economics of Scientific Journals*, edited by the Ad Hoc Committee on Economics of Publication. Bethesda, Md.: Council of Biology Editors, Inc., 1982.
6. King, Donald W., and Roderer, Nancy K. "Communication in Physics—the Use of Journals." *Physics Today* 35 (October 1982): 43–47.
7. McDonald, Dennis D. *Interactions between Scientists and the Journal Publishing Process*. Rockville, Md.: King Research, Inc., 1979.
8. Martin, M. D., comp. *Reference Manual for Machine-readable Bibliographic Descriptions*. SC74/WS/20. Paris: Unesco, 1974.
9. Dierickx, H., and Hopkinson, A., comps. and eds. *Reference Manual for Machine-readable Bibliographic Descriptions*. 2d ed. PGI/81/WS/22. Paris: Unesco, 1981.
10. King Research, Inc., for the National Commission on Library and Information Science. *Library Photocopying in the United States*. Washington, D.C.: Government Printing Office, October 1977.
11. Charles River Associates, Inc. *Development of a Model of the Demand for Scientific and Technical Information Services*. NTIS PB-297826. Boston: Charles River Associates, Inc., April 1979.
12. Lerner, Rita G.; Mick, Colin K.; and Callahan, Daniel. *Database Searching and Document Delivery via Communications Satellite*. NTIS PB81-153314. New York: American Institute of Physics, June 1980.
13. Norman, Adrian. *Electronic Document Delivery*. White Plains, N.Y.: Knowledge Industry Publications, 1981.
14. Feynman, Richard P. "There's Plenty of Room at the Bottom." *Engineering and Science Magazine* 23, no. 5 (February 1960): 22–26, 30–36.

PUBLISHERS AND LIBRARIANS: REFLECTIONS OF A RESEARCH LIBRARY ADMINISTRATOR

Jay K. Lucker[1]

In response to papers presented by several publishers, the author comments on the impact of photocopying, networking, and resource sharing on the acquisitions programs of research libraries. These practices are seen as having relatively little effect when compared with that of the availability of funds. The fiscal situation in academic institutions in general, and libraries in particular, is described with specific reference to the Massachusetts Institute of Technology libraries. Questions are raised about electronic publishing and the role of the research library as both subscriber and intermediary. Suggestions are made for improving communication between publishers and librarians.

This conference of publishers and librarians provides an opportunity not only to identify issues and problems that prevent the two groups from interacting more successfully but to exchange information that is necessary if they are to work together more closely in an uncertain future.

While my comments on the papers delivered by Lewis Coser [1], Morris Philipson [2], Frederick Praeger [3], Peter Urbach [4], and Rita Lerner [5] reflect my views in my principal role as the director of a large research library, I have had a number of responsibilities and experiences with the publishing field that, I believe, provide me with a balanced perspective. I have been an avid consumer of the output of both commercial and nonprofit publishers, with strong personal collecting and research interests in the history of science and technology. For the past seven years I have served on the editorial board of the MIT Press, reviewing publishing proposals with a major responsibility for advising the press on new journal projects. I have addressed various publishing groups, including the Society for Scholarly Publishing and the Scientific,

1. Office of the Director of Libraries, Massachusetts Institute of Technology, Room 14S-216, Cambridge, Massachusetts 02139.

Technical and Medical Publishers group of the Association of American Publishers (AAP). I have been an editor, a book reviewer, and sometimes an author.

Each of the previous speakers has addressed the general topic of the relationship between publishers and librarians from an individual perspective, but a number of themes are common to several of the papers. These topics—which I would summarize as concerns about the declining library market for scholarly publications; the impact of photocopying, networking, and resource sharing on the publishing industry; and the impact of current and future technological developments on publisher-library relations—provide the primary framework for my response. Before proceeding to these major issues, however, I would like to comment on a few other matters raised in the five preceding papers.

Morris Philipson questions whether there is general agreement on what a bookstore is, what a publisher is, or what a library is [2]. I feel unqualified to comment on the first two problems but respond to the third with the general reaction that libraries as we have known them are changing in both content and function. Libraries are beginning to accumulate information in formats that, in the past, have not been a major component of their holdings. Among the new (or recent) areas in which there have been significant increases are microforms, audiotapes and -disks, videotapes and -disks, machine-readable data, and optical video disks. Libraries are anticipating a future where ownership of information will decrease in importance and information will be more easily accessible, the library acting as intermediary. There is, indeed, a growing concern within the library community about libraries and librarians being "frozen out" of the new information age.

Philipson, as the director of a major university press, bemoans the effect of the reduced number of faculty and graduate students in the humanities and social sciences on the sale of scholarly monographs [2]. While it is likely that purchases of scholarly books by individual members of the academic community might well decline under such a situation, I see no direct correlation between this trend and research libraries' acquisition of university-press books. Simply stated, libraries must maintain research-level collections without much regard for the size of the faculty or graduate-student body. An acquisitions program costs about the same whether there are ten graduate students in a department or one hundred, assuming, as history has shown, that the breadth of subject interests barely declines even in a smaller research community. Maintaining high-level research collections in a period of declining enrollment is particularly difficult for research libraries whose materials budgets are computed on the basis on the number of students in each department. Graduate students seem to distribute themselves among all areas of specialization of an academic discipline much as faculty members do. Despite financial stringency and smaller student bodies, there has been little reduction in the number of different research and teaching interests in the average research university.

Lerner's comments about page charges lead me to make two comments [5]. First, the source of funds for some of these payments is often the general university budget, which is usually also the source for research library expenditures. Competition for general university funds is, as I will discuss later, one of the major fiscal trends of the 1970s and 1980s. Second, page charges are, in part, a subsidy paid by the research community for the publication of information. This is the same research community that relies heavily on library subscriptions for access to information; the price of subscriptions to journals published by scholarly societies is, more often than not, considerably higher for libraries than for individuals. To a research-university library director there is something here that defies logic!

Among the major concerns expressed by several of the publishers is the matter of library photocopying. Urbach [4], Lerner [5], and Praeger [3] all conclude that the photocopy machine in the hands of the librarian is the most serious threat to the survival of the publishing industry. Libraries are accused of photocopying books in lieu of ordering multiple copies and of substituting photocopying both internally and via interlibrary loan in place of institutional subscriptions. While I agree that there probably are instances of both these activities, they are hardly the normal way of life of academic libraries. Photocopying of entire books is both illegal and inane. It is illegal under the present copyright law and was illegal under its predecessor. Photocopying of whole books is also uneconomical if one considers both the cost of material and equipment and the cost of labor. Libraries, at least those with which I am familiar, continue to purchase multiple copies of books and to place them on reserve in response to faculty reading assignments. If libraries are buying fewer copies of Mr. Praeger's books, perhaps it is either because these books are not being assigned as required reading or, if they are, because libraries have sufficient copies.

An interesting change of direction has occurred in the relationship between the purchase of books by individual students and the purchase of books by libraries. With the advent of paperback scholarly publishing, faculty members, especially in the late 1960s and early 1970s, tended to require students to purchase more books, with a consequent reduction in library reserve purchases. The high rate of inflation that resulted in a greatly accelerated rate of tuition also resulted, however, in faculty concern about the additional burden on students of buying books for courses. There has been, therefore, a slow but steady reversal of the trend toward more student buying and fewer reserve assignments; this reversal, of course, places another burden on the already overburdened library materials budget.

In response to comments indicating that library photocopying has inhibited subscriptions to scholarly, scientific, and technical (SST) periodicals, I recommend that publishers and other interested parties analyze the data provided in the report prepared by King Research, Inc., for the U.S. Copyright Office entitled *Libraries, Publishers, and Photocopying* [6]. In commenting on this report to the Copyright Office, the Association of Research Libraries made the following statement:

The data provided by King Research strongly support the librarians' position, and offer no evidence of the consequences feared by the publisher interests concerned. For example:

A. The overall decrease of 16% in the number of copies of books, serials, and other materials made by library staff from 1976 to 1981 indicates that the present provisions are not too liberal from the standpoint of users, and that they have not encouraged wholesale photocopying, as was feared by publishers.

B. The growth of library consortia and networking arrangements does not seem to have been accompanied by the major increase of exchanges of photocopies. . . . The King data confirm that the preponderance of interlibrary loan (ILL) requests are still filled with originals. Depending upon which data are used, those filled with photocopies accounted for only 21% or 28% of all ILL requests. The data also demonstrate that there was only a modest 9% overall increase in the number of serial ILL requests filled with photocopies.

C. The evidence of the KRR [King Research report] on interlibrary loans is consistent with the libraries' 1975 testimony that it was their general experience that ILL encourages the entering of additional subscriptions by the library, rather than cancellation of existing subscriptions as often charged by the publishers. Indeed, 85.5% of SST journals and 90.7% of other serials either increased or maintained their circulation levels between 1976 and 1980. A substantial portion of these—45.6% and 39.6% respectively—increased in circulation. The KRR concludes that the library market for SST journals actually increased rather than decreased.

Serial publishers do not seem to have been constrained in their business decisions by the fears expressed by publishers at the Senate and House hearings. Indeed, the number of U.S. serial titles published in 1980 was 21% greater than the 1976 output. Approximately 6,100 new serial titles were started after 1976, while 1,800 were discontinued, representing an overall birth-to-death ratio of about 3.4 to 1. The growth rate for SST journals was 31% with a birth-to-death ratio of 3.8 to 1. These data show that library photocopying is not being done in lieu of subscriptions. [7, pp. 4-13 to 4-14]

My skepticism about the impact of photocopying on subscriptions is further advanced by data from my own institution. In the past academic year, July 1, 1981, through June 30, 1982, the Massachusetts Institute of Technology libraries circulated approximately 500,000 items through several circulation desks. Having used a number of samples, we believe that the rate of in-house circulation—that is, the use of books and

journals within the libraries that is not represented by circulation transactions—is about twice that of external circulation. The total circulation
for MIT last year was, therefore, about 1,500,000. The total number of
interlibrary borrowing transactions—requests made to other libraries by
MIT for MIT students, faculty, and research staff—was 4,000, of which
about 25 percent, or 1,000, were photocopies. The ratio of interlibrary
loans to total loans (1:400) or of photocopies requested to total loans
(1:1500) leads me to suggest that there is some exaggeration in the
notion that libraries are using interlibrary-loan photocopying to excess.

One reaction I have to some of the comments about photocopying in
libraries can be summarized: The answer is photocopying! What is the
question?

Is it: (1) What raises the ire of publishers and causes them to make
outlandish and exaggerated statements? (2) What provides scholars with
a quick and inexpensive means of acquiring information, much of it
representing their own *free* contributions as authors, editors, referees,
directors of societies, and payers of page charges? or (3) What do
libraries do in accordance with the copyright law that is so misunder-
stood by publishers?

Another recurring theme in the papers presented by the publishers at
this conference is that resource sharing and networking have been major
factors in the declining market for scholarly publications. While I do
agree that the market for scholarly publications has been shrinking and
will continue to shrink, particularly in research libraries, I believe
strongly that it is the availability of acquisitions funds—a matter that I
will expound on shortly—and not networks or resource sharing or the
adoption of computers that will be the principal cause.

Libraries are the primary market for scholarly publications and a
major market for the output of other types of publishing. In addition to
acquiring books, periodicals, and other materials, these institutions serve
as a means of publicizing new books and in that way reinforce the lines
of communication between the publisher and the individual scholar.
While it is true that book reviews and displays in bookstores sell books,
one should not overlook the possibility of reaching prospective buyers
through their use of or exposure to a particular item in a library. It is my
firm belief that a significant number of individual subscriptions to scholarly, scientific, and technical journals, as well as to general periodicals,
are generated by the prior existence of those titles in academic, public,
and special libraries. Academic and research libraries are not only the
major market for scholarly materials; they are often the only market. I
would suggest that for the following types of materials, libraries support
the publication costs and profit (if any) almost entirely on their own: (1)
abstracting and indexing services such as *Chemical Abstracts* and *Biological*

Abstracts (how many individual subscribers are there today to *CA* at nearly $10,000 per year?); (2) large multivolume reference works such as the collected papers of Presidents Wilson and Jefferson or the *Encyclopaedic Dictionary of Physics* [8]; (3) statistical volumes and other annuals; (4) specialized journals in disciplines with small professional populations; and (5) major microform publications such as *Landmarks of Science* [9].

Cooperation among libraries has, of course, increased tremendously in the past two decades. One of the most impressive demonstrations of library cooperation, particularly as it relates to the shared cataloging of acquired materials, has been OCLC, Inc., the Online Computer Library Center. Through a system of networks, libraries throughout the country are able, first, to utilize the machine-readable cataloging produced by the Library of Congress (LC), and second, to share the cataloging of books and other items not cataloged by LC that members place into the system. Cost savings to member institutions have been substantial, particularly in the area of staff, but there has been another benefit in having the OCLC database. The ability to identify the existence of a particular item in a particular library has greatly improved the speed and quality of interlibrary-loan service in the United States. I must say, however, that the use of the OCLC system for interlibrary loans—for both identification of location and transmission of request—has not significantly affected the acquisitions policies of member libraries. I am aware of no major academic library that makes decisions about whether to acquire items for its collections on the basis of their location in another library, except in cases where there have been prior agreements on shared collection development. These prior agreements are usually built around the concept of sharing responsibility for the acquisition of very expensive materials, especially those in very specialized subjects. In general, I would argue that acquisitions decisions are being made today principally on the basis of cost and relevance to the academic and research programs and not on the basis of the availability of the particular item in another library.

Librarians have long espoused resource sharing as a means of cooperation among libraries, but relatively few substantive demonstrations have been made among the major academic and research libraries. The principal reasons are philosophical and technical. In the former category of reasons is that of the matter of local availability. Faculty, graduate students, and upper-level undergraduates have been unwilling to forgo local availability for bibliographic identification and remote location. On the technical side, while we have the means to identify the library or libraries owning a particular item, we still rely on relatively slow means of whole-text delivery. I do believe we will see more cooperative use of collections, but for the immediate future this cooperation will be in the areas of older collections of research materials or very specialized subjects.

I can see the development of networks as having a positive rather than a negative effect on acquisitions. When libraries can cooperate more efficiently in performing such functions as cataloging, ordering, and circulation, for example, they may find it possible to reduce the costs associated with these operations and thus release much-needed funds for acquisitions. The real problem is how to squeeze more acquisitions dollars out of budgets that are not increasing as quickly as the rate of inflation is or that, in many cases, are not increasing at all.

Comments made by previous speakers at this conference lead me to believe that there is less than full understanding of the nature of the current fiscal situation in academic libraries, particularly those serving large research universities. To see how we got to where we are, it seems useful to trace the fiscal situation as it has developed over the past decade.

During the 1970s, academic institutions could be characterized as having to deal with a number of challenges. Revenues were essentially level. It was necessary to maintain enrollments at their then-current levels. Increased funding, however, was needed for recruitment and student aid and for the introduction of popular new courses and fields (for example, business administration, law, computer science, medical technology). In response, there was a great deal of cost cutting that was accomplished in three ways: (1) little economies—reduced energy use, shortened library hours, reduced faculty travel and research assistance, cancelled institutional memberships, elimination of football, use of more part-time faculty, shortened academic year; (2) deferred maintenance and replacement of assets; and (3) reduced "real" compensation of staff members and faculty (by not keeping up with inflation).

Several results of these actions became evident toward the end of the period; many of these still haunt us today: (1) deferred maintenance of buildings, grounds, and equipment; (2) deferred replacement of worn-out or obsolete assets; (3) drawing down of reserves; (4) use for current operations of gifts that should have gone into endowment; (5) failure to keep library collections up to date; (6) failure to maintain inventories; (7) failure to purchase new equipment to keep pace with changing technologies; and (8) loss of academic talent to business, industry, and government due to failure to maintain compensation levels.

The overall quality of education has also been affected by other factors not so directly related to the economic stringencies of the 1970s: (1) increased size of educational institutions, which has led to a growing bureaucracy; (2) increased numbers of part-time and commuting stu-

TABLE 1

Total MIT Libraries Expenditures for Library
Materials, 1970–81

Year	Current Dollars	Constant Dollars*
1970	428,773	428,773
1971	563,290	536,467
1972	586,344	537,930
1973	606,797	523,101
1974	691,783	544,711
1975	730,192	529,125
1976	758,574	519,571
1977	829,355	549,242
1978	972,752	604,166
1979	1,121,652	645,249
1980	1.302,775	690,413
1981	1,421,203	691,793

Sources.—MIT libraries budgets, 1970–81; [11, p. 459].
*GNP deflator, 1970 = 100.

dents; (3) more part-time and nontenured faculty; and (4) greater emphasis on vocational interests of students and on responsiveness to the job market [10].

The principal factor affecting library budgets in the past fifteen years has been a rise in the cost of materials at a rate that tends to be consistently greater than that of the Consumer Price Index. Tables 1 and 2 document the impact of this inflation on the budget of the MIT libraries. Table 1 shows the effects of inflation on the total materials budget, table 2 on the serials portion of that budget. Serials rose in cost at a rate much greater than that of general prices.

The evidence from table 1 shows, depressingly, that, while expenditures for library materials at MIT rose by a factor of 3.3 from 1970 through 1981, the value of that increase in constant dollars was a factor of only 1.6. Table 2 shows that serial expenditures rose, in the period 1970 through 1982, by a factor of 5.1 but the tremendous inflation in serial prices during the same period produced, by the end of the period, a budget that was essentially able to cover roughly the same amount of serial acquisitions.

Other economic factors having a major impact on research libraries include:

a) The decreasing amount of federal support for student aid, scholarships, and graduate fellowships has placed a severe burden on institutional budgets and has caused the diverting of funds from other activities, including libraries.

b) Through 1983, there was a decrease in federal support for basic

TABLE 2
TOTAL MIT LIBRARIES SERIAL EXPENDITURES, 1970–82

Year	Current Dollars	Constant Dollars*
1970	208,788	173,990
1971	262,778	196,102
1972	304,330	198,908
1973	301,314	161,130
1974	381,999	186,340
1975	442,734	192,493
1976	466,846	179,556
1977	530,294	186,723
1978	614,883	193,725
1979	685,273	195,662
1980	834,307	204,858
1981	911,574	185,806
1982	1,054,239	171,870

SOURCES.—MIT libraries budgets, 1970–82; [12, p. 1380].
*U.S. Periodical Index, 1967–69 = 100.

research at research universities. The indirect cost support provided by such research forms a significant portion of most research library budgets.

c) Federal funding for academic libraries has decreased substantially during the past ten years, especially under the Title II-A program of the Higher Education Act. Title II-C of that act has been funded at a steady level but never at the level authorized in the enabling legislation. Other federal programs that benefit academic libraries more indirectly, such as LSCA and Title II-B, have been severely curtailed.

d) Changes in the retirement laws have reduced staff turnover and have resulted in the retention of staff with longer service and higher salaries.

e) Various sets of government regulations have placed additional financial burdens on colleges and universities in compliance, record-keeping, reviews, and hearings. While some of these, such as affirmative action and occupational health and safety, are politically and socially desirable, other changes in such areas as indirect cost recovery and information transfer seem less useful and are more expensive to carry out.

f) The amount of capital available to adapt to technological change has decreased.

g) The financial base of many institutions has shifted. Tuition is now the principal source of income, and other sources, such as continuing education and applied research, are being pursued.

h) There has been a lack of growth in endowment in terms of both principal and interest.

i) Tax laws have decreased the incentive to give money to educational institutions.

j) Foundations have been less inclined to provide funds for bricks and mortar or for endowment. Support for libraries has been more in the area of national programs—which, of course, is quite important.

k) There has been a shift from federal to state support of many discretionary programs, including higher education.

l) The increased cost of higher education, along with general inflation, has placed more of a direct burden on libraries (for example, faculty members place books on reserve rather than requiring students to buy them; faculty also cancel personal subscriptions and purchase fewer books for their personal libraries).

In attempting to explain why it has been difficult for libraries to increase or even maintain a level of acquisitions that would provide publishers with a less pessimistic view of the present and future, one must also consider some of the peculiarities and limitations of library budgets: (1) the substantial portion allocated to personnel; (2) the compartmentalized nature of library operations; (3) the high cost of making changes and the slow rate at which these changes can be accomplished; (4) the fact that the principal source of income is almost always the institutional appropriation (other sources, such as endowment, gifts, grants, income from fees, charges, and services, represent a much smaller percentage of income); (5) the extremely high fixed costs of maintaining a large storehouse of information; (6) the large expense of maintaining aging collections; (7) the fact that the introduction of new technology seldom reduces operating costs; (8) the proportionally increased cost of providing service as collections grow; (9) the fact that those who benefit from the services and collections are seldom in a decision-making position concerning the budget; and (10) the difficulty of demonstrating the value of a library except when services or collections are reduced.

Another area that has received considerable attention during this conference has been publishing in general and electronic publishing in particular. I was deeply intrigued by the predictions of Peter Urbach [4] and the plan of the American Institute of Physics as presented by Rita Lerner [5]. While, as a research library administrator, I am fully prepared to operate in an environment where the printed journal as we know it will cease to exist, or even one where only some journals are published electronically, I do have concerns about how libraries will function in this changing situation.

In assessing the potential impact of electronic publishing, one can select one of two assumptions regarding the options that libraries will have for access. Simply stated, they are either electronic only or electronic and print. These two possibilities will, however, create a most interesting quandary for research libraries. If journals are published only in electronic form, it would seem logical for libraries to divert expenditures formerly applied to print versions to the new format. If, however, both electronic and print versions are available, libraries will most probably continue to subscribe to the older format, creating a situation where the user may have to pay for an individual article generated by an electronic-journal data bank. Should the latter situation prevail, faculty members and students will inevitably have to make a choice whether to purchase an article electronically or rely on the library subscription for information. This choice would probably be made on the basis of speed of delivery and cost, assuming the availability of funds.

Librarians have a number of questions regarding electronic-journal publication. One asks how individual articles will be priced when total sales obviously cannot be gauged in advance; this situation compares unfavorably with traditional methods of pricing journals based on total projected costs and advance subscriptions. A second matter of interest is the impact on cost of the loss of advertising, an assumption that is probably valid in most scenarios.

Should the electronic-only option be adopted, it seems likely that libraries, assuming they would serve as the principal ordering agent for articles, would provide the article to the user for retention rather than maintain a file of "ordered and received articles." The beneficial effects of such a system on what publishers view as a copyright problem should be apparent. Another matter of concern is the need for quick and comprehensive abstracting tools that would replace the current browsing of tables of contents. With the absence of immediate access to the source document, users will want more substantial information than normally appears in titles. Synoptic abstracts, possibly available online, preferably prepared by the author, and ideally distributed in a subject-oriented collection, seem highly desirable.

Several other issues seem relevant at this point. First, access to information by libraries and their users will become increasingly more attractive than ownership, especially for current scientific and technical research, but the existence of an excellent and reasonably priced delivery system is imperative. Second, electronic journals do not necessarily have to contain full back files of articles for extended periods. It is conceivable that the electronic journal online would contain only the five most recent years of articles with earlier collections converted to microfiche and sold by subscription to libraries (and individuals). Indeed, if economic viability is to be achieved, it appears essential that only a limited online file be maintained. Third, as members of the academic community, librarians share with their faculty colleagues concerns about electronic-journal publishing and scholarly research that have to do with the publication of work in progress as well as completed research. If work in progress is to be published, will there be the danger of premature exposure of research results and will scholarly journals (the conventional kind) be less willing to publish the later version? How will articles be refereed if they appear only in electronic form? Will scholars be willing to referee online? What about access to terminals? Will there be a tendency to publish everything because of the comparative ease of publication?

From the perspective of peer evaluation, other questions must be considered. Will electronic publication be seen as publishing (for promotion and tenure decisions)? What if no one ever requests a particular article? Is this some measure of scholarly attainment? Is there a danger that frequency of purchase of an article will be viewed as some institutions now view frequency of citation? Will publishers report sales of individual articles, and if so, to whom? Only to the author? Will prices of individual articles rise astronomically given the fact that there are relatively few readers of the average article? Conversely, will only articles with a large, known audience appear in the electronic journal?

While the question of the possible lack of advertising was raised earlier on economic grounds, librarians also have serious concerns from the intellectual point of view. Advertisements, especially in scientific and technical journals, often contain important information about scientific apparatus and about new books and other publications. Indeed, what will happen to features of scholarly journals like book reviews, letters to the editor, and obituaries? Who will buy these items, and, more important, who will pay to have them "published"?

Finally, if all this were not enough to worry about, librarians (and scholars) should also be concerned about the linkage of electronic journals with online bibliographic databases, the role of the library and the librarian in both the publication and the dissemination aspects of electronic publishing, the question of international access to journal databases and the concomitant question of telecommunication across national boundaries, and the need for standardization of formats for access protocols and of hardware.

There are a number of areas where publishers and librarians could begin to work together more closely and more effectively. First of all, it might be useful to talk about some practices of publishers that both irritate and mystify librarians. These practices include the discriminatory pricing of journals with rates for libraries anywhere from two to ten times greater than individual subscriptions; the repackaging of information under the subterfuge of "new editions," anthologies, collected papers, and the like; overadvertising that results in libraries receiving what seems like an infinite number of flyers and brochures for the same item; "phony" series that seem to have been designed solely to confuse librarians so that they place unnecessary standing orders; and books printed on poor paper and bound in such a way as to guarantee disintegration after only a few uses.

On a more substantive note I recommend that publishers consider consulting librarians to find out what kinds of reference books we do not have that we need; using microfiche instead of print for voluminous statistical information, tables, charts, and so forth; publishing statistical information in machine-readable form; using librarians in an advisory capacity on publishing and editorial boards, especially for those organizations for whom libraries represent a major portion of the market; seeking the advice of librarians when considering the publication of a new journal to find out if the title is really needed.

A large number of issues divide publishers and librarians, but we also have a great deal in common in our joint goal to increase the dissemination of knowledge. The dissemination of knowledge, after all, is one of the three main purposes of a university, along with the preservation of knowledge and the creation of new knowledge. A future without publishers or libraries seems totally unreasonable, not to say impossible. This conference has been an important and significant event in the development of understanding between the two groups, and I look forward with happy anticipation to future collaboration and cooperation.

REFERENCES

1. Coser, Lewis A. "The Publishing Industry as a Hybrid." In this issue.
2. Philipson, Morris. "Intrinsic Value versus Market Value." In this issue.
3. Praeger, Frederick A. "Librarians, Publishers, and Scholars, Common Interests, Different Views: The View of an Independent Scholarly Publisher." In this issue.
4. Urbach, Peter. "The View of a For-Profit Scientific Publisher." In this issue.
5. Lerner, Rita G. "The Professional Society in a Changing World." In this issue.
6. McDonald, Dennis D., and Bush, Colleen G., with King, Donald W., et al. *Libraries, Publishers, and Photocopying: Final Report of Surveys Conducted for the United States Copyright Office.* Rockville, Md.: King Research Co., 1982.
7. Association of Research Libraries. *Comments to the Copyright Office.* Washington, D.C.: Association of Research Libraries, 1982.
8. *Encyclopaedic Dictionary of Physics: General, Nuclear, Solid State, Molecular, Chemical, Metal and Vacuum Physics, Astronomy, Geophysics, Biophysics and Related Subjects.* New York: Pergamon Press, 1961.
9. Cohen, I. Bernard, ed. *Landmarks of Science.* New York: Readex Microprint, 1967–.
10. Minter, John, and Bowen, Howard R. "The Minter-Bowen Report, Part I." *Chronicle of Higher Education* 26 (May 12, 1982): 5–7.
11. *Statistical Abstract of the United States, 1981.* Washington, D.C.: Government Printing Office, 1981.
12. Brown, Norman B., and Phillips, Jane. "Price Indexes of 1982." *Library Journal* 107 (August 1982): 1379–82.

THE SMALL BOOK PRESS: A CULTURAL ESSENTIAL

Bill Henderson[1]

Small book presses are flourishing in this country as never before. Today's presses publish books on a variety of subjects, but the focus of this paper is on the small literary book publisher. Small presses are alternatives to the commercial establishment, issuing works that larger publishers avoid for commercial or editorial reasons. A small press might be operated by a single, self-publishing author, a group of friends, or a collective; about 2,700 such presses are currently active. "Vanity" presses are not the same as small presses and are held in disrepute. Authors in the small-press tradition include Thomas Paine, Washington Irving, Walt Whitman, Mark Twain, Upton Sinclair, and Anaïs Nin. Among today's outstanding presses are the Creative Arts Book Company, Persea Books, Full Court Press, the Reed and Cannon Company, and Tuumba Books. Little magazines—often published by small book presses—are important to book publication because they encourage the new talents that literary book presses—both small and large—publish.

If small literary presses had not begun to flourish in the 1960s and 1970s and were not continuing to prosper in the current decade, very little imaginative writing would be published in this country. Serious fiction, poetry, the inventive essay—all would find few outlets beyond a few commercial magazines and a handful of book houses. It is a tribute to our democracy and the will of writers and editors that our literature has not died out—despite a culture devoted to television sitcoms, rock stars, and disposable best-sellers. Indeed, not since the Paris of Hemingway, Pound, and Joyce has so much talent been invested in small presses. Today's small press, however, is often not just a literary enterprise. Its books and journals may specialize in a variety of subjects, including child care, car repair, photography, even earthworm farming. But this paper will concentrate on the most important function of today's small presses—the preservation and advancement of creative literature. My focus will be on book publication.

1. Pushcart Press, P.O. Box 380, Wainscott, New York 11975.

First, a few definitions are needed. A small press is a publisher of books or periodicals, or both, that is run by from one person to a collective of many voices. It specializes in the publication of literary materials that commercial publishers the size of Doubleday and Company or McGraw-Hill Book Company—or magazine companies like *Cosmopolitan* or *Playboy*—find of no interest for financial and/or editorial reasons. A small press is an alternative to the commercial establishment. Often the press can be a profit-making alternative (especially if it concentrates now and then on practical and specialized publications), but usually, for the literary publisher, profit is of minimal interest. What matters most is the creative work. Self-publication is similar to small-press publication, but in self-publication the author writes, edits, and sometimes prints and distributes his or her own work. Self-publication provides an author the means to reach the public by investing personal funds and effort.

Self-publishing and small-press publishing should never be confused with "vanity" publishing. The vanity press is deservedly held in disrepute by both commercial and small presses, for it publishes anything for which an author will pay, usually at a loss for the author and a nice profit for the publisher. The vanity publisher entices the author with promises of advertisements and reviews, but reviews are rarely obtained—because reviewers shun vanity-press books—and advertisements are crammed together in blocks. After so-called publication, vanity-press books usually remain in the publisher's warehouse until they are pulped. The author almost never receives money in return. In contrast, the self-publishing author is able to promote and peddle the work honestly and if successful gain the rewards.

A small press is not the same as a small publisher. A small press is run by fewer people and produces fewer titles a year; if it produces a little magazine, that magazine has a circulation that ranges from 2 to 10,000 copies, the average being somewhere between 500 and 3,000. A small publisher, on the other hand, may issue dozens of titles a year and employ a staff of many people; if it is a magazine company, it may boast a circulation of up to 100,000 copies. Also, a small publisher, with a larger overhead and staff to support, is much more interested in the bottom line than a small press is and thus is less likely to experiment or take chances on new talent and unusual ideas.

While small literary presses may be the cultural saviors of our time, their numbers may baffle the average reader and exasperate the librarian trying to keep track of their comings and goings. Each year Pushcart Press invites all small presses in existence to make nominations of poetry, fiction, and essays for the annual *Pushcart Prize* anthology [1], and approximately 2,700 such presses are currently active. Many presses that exist, however, may not be active in a given year. They may have issued 1 book or 1 copy of a little magazine, lost their enthusiasm or bank balances, and quit. They may have invested their all in single projects and afterwards gone into hibernation, awaiting sales returns on their investments. They may exist only as a letterhead or on hope. But the mere fact that they have announced their births means that Pushcart contacts them and that they are listed in the reference bible of the small presses—*The International Directory of Little Magazines and Small Presses* [2].

This directory is the crucial reference tool for any library that wants to provide its acquisitions department and its patrons with current information on active or would-be presses. Other useful tools are the *Book Publishers Directory* [3] and the *Small Press Record of Books in Print* [4]. The annual *Pushcart Prize* anthology, which reprints about fifty selected poems, essays, and short stories and provides a listing of active presses with addresses, might serve as a secondary reference tool to these volumes.

For reviews of small-press publications there are unfortunately few reliable and professional sources. *Library Journal* remains the one magazine that attempts to review just about all books or periodicals of interest to libraries. *Booklist* is also very useful. *Publishers Weekly* often reviews small-press books of a general interest, as does *Kirkus Reviews* from time to time. Journals like *Small Press Review* may be helpful if consulted along with the review resources just named.

The small press, whether functioning as a book publisher, a self-publisher, or a little magazine, has performed an important function in American literary history. The following examples illustrate both the function and the potential of independent presses.

One of the first and most important small presses in the United States was run by the printer Robert Bell and the author Thomas Paine, with the advice and encouragement of the physician Benjamin Rush. When the press's first publication, *Common Sense* [5], came out on January 10, 1776, not many people were seriously considering independence from England. Six months later, largely because of the essays in this pamphlet, the Declaration of Independence was signed. Paine originally thought of having his essays published as a series of letters to the editors of colonial newspapers, but most editors would not print them. At the urging of Dr. Rush, Paine and Bell decided to publish his collected essays at two shillings a copy in a first edition of 1,000 copies. The first printing sold out in two weeks. By 1779, 150,000 copies had been sold, and total sales reached over 500,000 copies [6, p. 15].

On October 26, 1809, the *New York Evening Post* printed a notice that read: "Distressing—Left his lodgings some time since and has not since been heard of, a small elderly gentleman, dressed in an old black coat and cocked hat, by the name of Knickerbocker." A notice in the *Post* of November 6 reported that such a man had been seen a little above Kingsbridge by passengers of the Albany stage. In the November 16 *Post,* Seth Handaside, landlord of the Columbian Hotel, announced "a very curious kind of written book has been found in his room, in his own handwriting. Now I wish you to notice him if he is alive that if he does not return and pay off his bill for boarding and lodging, I shall have to dispose of the book to satisfy me for the same."

Using this hoax as an advertising device, Washington Irving, with the help of friends, publicized *A History of New York* by Diedrich Knickerbocker, Irving's pen name [7]. The book was printed in Philadelphia in order to preserve the mystery in New York. After the advance publicity, the 2-volume work, priced at three dollars, appeared in New York bookshops [8, p. 96]. Irving was later acclaimed America's first man of letters and the *History* called "the first great book of comic literature by an American" [8, p. 96].

Walt Whitman is the champion of American do-it-yourself publishers. In 1855 he personally set the type for *Leaves of Grass* [9] on a press in Brooklyn, New York—95 pages, 12 poems, somewhat under 1,000 books. He got his review copies out and attracted some notice, but he wrote the best reviews himself in the *Brooklyn Times,* the *American Phrenological Journal,* and the *United States and Democratic Review.* Reviewer Whitman described himself as "of pure American breed, large and lusty . . . , a naive, masculine, affectionate, contemplative, sensual, imperious person" [10, p. 147].

The copy Whitman sent to Ralph Waldo Emerson brought less prejudiced praise. Whitman recognized the value of the letter and, without Emerson's permission, splashed in gold on the back of his next self-published edition in 1856 [11]: "I greet you at the beginning of a great career—Emerson." This edition included Emerson's letter in full in an appendix that was devoted to reviews of the first edition, an edition that Whitman bragged had sold out. This sales figure was not quite true. The 1855 edition had been placed in a bookstore, but when the bookseller bothered to read the poems, he judged them morally objectionable and ordered Whitman to get them off his shelves. Whitman took them to a store that specialized in volumes on phrenology, the water cure, and vegetarianism, but few copies were sold there either. Whitman gave away many copies and sold the rest for pennies apiece to a remainder dealer. The next edition, 21 poems longer, fared no better; reviewers were outraged by Whitman's sexual references. Emerson pleaded with Whitman to tone down his work, but Whitman refused.

In 1860 Whitman found his first commercial publisher, Thayer and

Eldridge of Boston. The firm sold 4,000 copies of *Leaves of Grass* [12] at $1.25 each and then went bankrupt. However, Whitman's international reputation was growing. In 1868 a 28-page edition appeared in England, and other editions were published on the Continent. Meanwhile, Whitman self-published 2 more editions in 1867 and 1871, losing money on both.

A stroke in 1873 left Whitman in failing health but did little to affect his publishing spirits. He recuperated at his brother's home in Camden, New Jersey, and busied himself with writing and filling orders. He may have written the article in the *West Jersey Press* of January 26, 1876, that described him as "old, poor, paralysed" and neglected by his ungrateful countrymen. No matter who wrote it, Whitman sent it to friends in England, and an international furor developed that boosted sales. With his full beard and his basket of books, Whitman became a familiar sight about Camden—poet, self-printer, self-publisher, and delivery boy. Recognizing his sales possibilities, the Boston firm of James B. Osgood decided to venture an edition. They had sold 1,600 copies when the Boston Society for Suppression of Vice howled about court action. Osgood asked Whitman to change a few words, received a flat refusal, and stopped publishing. Whitman persevered, self-publishing an autographed, 300-copy limited edition in 1889 [13] and a final volume in 1892 [14] that was distributed by David McKay Company as the poet lay on his deathbed [6, p. 23].

Whitman had saved his book from obscurity and outwitted the vice committees by his promotional skill—although he did not get rich on profits from his work.

Mark Twain, while hardly the underdog, was also published by his own small press. He formed the press in 1885, with his nephew, Charles L. Webster, to publish *Huckleberry Finn* [15]. The name "Mark Twain" was already a household word, and he expected, correctly, that he would profit from the venture. Twain and his nephew sold a creditable 40,000 copies of *Huckleberry Finn* by subscription in advance of publication. After the publication date, Twain received an unexpected publicity break when the Concord, Massachusetts, public library banned his novel. Twain exulted, "That will sell 25,000 copies of our book for sure!" Total sales amounted to more than 500,000 copies.

Later, Twain and his nephew published other books with varying success. His most important project was Ulysses S. Grant's *Memoirs* [16], which sold 312,000 sets at nine dollars per set. Twain gave Grant's widow a whopping 70 percent royalty. His generosity caused the press to end in disaster in 1894, and he labored for four years on a world lecture circuit to pay off his debts [6].

The small presses of Paris during the twentieth century are legendary, but at the same time many American independents were doing important work. A typical publishing story is that involving the publication of Upton Sinclair's *The Jungle* [17]. "Too much blood and guts," a commercial house said when rejecting *The Jungle*. The author refused to compromise. After five rejections, he and his friends formed an independent group to publish the book. Jack London contributed a manifesto calling on the socialist movement in New York to rally to the novel.

Sinclair ran a prepublication subscription for *The Jungle* and, at $1.20 per copy, raised $4,000—more money than he had earned in his first five years of writing. The novel was in type, waiting for the press to roll, when Doubleday and Page happened along in 1906 and offered to publish a simultaneous edition [18]. The novel reached the stomachs of the entire nation and ensured the passage of the Pure Food and Drug Acts. Sinclair continued to publish through his own press when commercial publishers rejected his sometimes socially controversial work in the future [6, p. 30].

Carl Sandburg's first collection of poems, *In Reckless Ecstasy* [19], was published in 1904 by the Asgard Press, the small press of Sandburg's professor, Philip Green Wright, at Lombard College, Galesburg, Illinois. Wright, a poet himself, founded a club at Lombard, the Poor Writer's Club, where Sandburg and a few other students met weekly to read their own creations and those of established authors. Wright's edition of *In Reckless Ecstasy* was printed in the basement of Wright's home. The 50-copy, 50-page edition was bound in cardboard and held together with ribbon. A copy is now worth five hundred dollars [6, p. 31].

Anaïs Nin arrived in New York in the winter of 1939. Her novel *Winter of Artifice* [20] was published in Paris but, because of the war, received no distribution or reviews. When American publishers refused the book, she and her friend Gonzalo More bought a second-hand printing press and rented a studio in Greenwich Village to do the job. She describes the start of her press in her diary: "The creation of an individual world, an act of independence, such as the work at the press, is a marvelous cure for anger and frustration. The insults of the publishers, the rejections, the ignorance, all are forgotten" [21, p. 18]. She recalls working and sleeping at the press with ink in her food, hair, and nails. Finally *Winter of Artifice* was printed and published at the Gotham Book Mart (New York) in May 1941. More and Nin then published other work they admired. But even though the press was constantly threatened by financial problems, they continued for over a decade, sustained by the praise of friends and reviewers [21, p. 35].

Small-press publication continued throughout the 1950s, introducing underground literature—particularly the work of Beats like Allen Ginsberg and Lawrence Ferlinghetti—to a literary audience that would never have heard of them if publication had been left to commercial houses. But it was during the 1960s that the small-press tradition grew from a few scattered operations into what might be called a movement. Typical of the spirit of these times was the publication of Barbara Garson's *MacBird* [22] by a Berkeley, California, collective. Garson and the collective first issued the play, a satirical attack on Lyndon Johnson, during the early days of the Vietnam war. The collective sold 100,000 copies in paperback at a dollar a copy by hawking them around the campus of the University of California, Berkeley [23]. Eventually the play was produced on Broadway and sold another 300,000 copies in a Grove Press edition [24].

Another 1960s collective success was *Foxfire*. In 1966, Eliot Wigginton, a teacher in Rabun Gap, Georgia, and his pupils decided to put together a journal about food, literature, customs, and crafts. Neither the teacher nor the pupils had any money, so they hounded contributors and gathered four hundred and fifty dollars to print the first issue of *Foxfire*. To fund later issues they appealed to the Coordinating Council of Literary Magazines (CCLM), a nonprofit funding organization that received funds from the National Endowment for the Arts; they were awarded direct and matching grants that enabled them to keep *Foxfire* alive. Later on, Doubleday's Anchor Press issued the first 2 volumes of the journal as book anthologies [25–31]. These books sold millions of copies in various editions, but the world would never have heard of *Foxfire* and its down-home traditions if it had not been for the spirit of Wigginton and his student collective [32].

As in the publication of *Foxfire*, the National Endowment for the Arts' literature program and its affiliates like CCLM became increasingly important throughout the 1970s. Concern also arose that federal financing deprived small presses of much of their maverick status, not through any government censorship demands but through self-censorship as the presses competed for grants.

During the 1960s and early 1970s, hundreds of presses started and folded in a brief time, but many are still with us and doing very well. Len Fulton's Dustbooks, which publishes the *International Directory of Little Magazines and Small Presses*, got its start in the mid-1960s. A little later, David Godine started business in Boston as a fine book printer. His printing shop expanded into publishing, and the firm of David R. Godine, Publisher, is now widely noted not only for the quality of its list but also for the craftsmanship of its book production. Too often small-press publications are sloppy and slapdash. Godine—carrying on in the tradition of England's nineteenth-century master printer, William Morris—publishes editions that are works of art in themselves.

It would be impossible to consider in depth the thousands of presses that have come and gone in the past two decades and the approximately 2,700 presses listed as active in the current Dustbooks directory [2]. These presses issue work that ranges from the noble to the slapstick, from the enlightened to the outer fringe of sanity. But a few examples drawn from today's small book press scene might help those trying to understand how these presses produce and market their books.

The Creative Arts Book Company is located in Berkeley, California— the most popular center for today's small presses. Creative Arts produces up to 8 new titles a year, divided between reprints and originals. It has issued works by Gertrude Stein, William Saroyan, E. M. Forster, Aldous Huxley, Frank O'Hara, and others. In order to pay the bills, Creative Arts also publishes nonfiction titles of everyday practical interest, such as *The Avocado Cookbook* [33]. Creative Arts has published 43 titles since it started in 1976, and 40 of those titles are still in print: a virtue of most small presses is that, unlike the commercial giants, they will not pulp or remainder slow-selling books. Creative Arts sells its books through all major and minor wholesalers and through the efforts of twelve commissioned sales representatives. Says publisher Don Ellis, "We don't have a private fortune to guarantee our survival: we have to make money, or at least break even in order to continue; and as long as the public continues to read good books, we'll be around" [34, p. 40].

New York City, the second major home for small presses, is the location of Persea Books, run by Michael Braziller from a one-room office in the East Village. Braziller's press, existing on a shoestring budget and no grants, publishes a distinguished list of fiction, nonfiction, poetry, and translations. Persea warehouses and ships its books through a company in Staten Island, is represented in bookstores by a team of commissioned representatives, and also distributes titles published by Joyce Carol Oates's Ontario Review Press, the Sheep Meadow Press, and several others.

Another New York City publisher is Full Court Press, founded by Joan Simon, Ron Padgett, and Anne Waldman to issue "a variety of works we thought not only ought to be in print but should also stay there" [35]. Full Court both introduces new writers and publishes established authors such as William Carlos Williams and Allen Ginsberg. All of its books are produced simultaneously in paper, cloth, and signed limited editions. Full Court makes no distinction between front- and backlist and hopes all its books continue to sell steadily. The press also issues a Rebound series—books that other publishers were about to pulp or to declare out of print. Full Court sells these titles in the original editions, and, unlike remainder dealers, it continues to pay full royalties to the author and to reprint the books when stocks run out. Full Court reaches its buyers through direct mail and sells to bookstores and libraries directly and through wholesalers. The press exhibits at all trade and small-press book fairs and, like other presses, depends heavily on word of mouth to promote its titles.

The Reed and Cannon Company, founded in 1973 by Ishmael Reed with Steven Cannon, is unique in providing a home for Third World voices. "As long as people are prevented from experiencing a diversity of literature, they will be incapable of coping with an international society. The white European tradition is not the only tradition," says Reed, who is also the author of several acclaimed novels [36, p. 31]. Reed's original publications were the five *Yardbird Reader* magazines, each containing scores of poems, stories, and essays by Asian-, Hispanic-, and Afro-Americans. In recent years, Reed and Cannon have issued books under various imprints. Reed also started the Before Columbus Foundation to sell the books of sixty-five other Third World publishers.

It would be fitting to close this brief sampling of presses with a one-woman enterprise that represents the spirit of so many other do-it-yourself presses. Lyn Hejinian is the only employee at her Tuumba Press. She is Tuumba's editor, designer, typesetter, and printer. The only assistance she receives comes from her family—she is the mother of two teenagers—when it is time for her books to be packaged and mailed. Her Berkeley, California, home serves as her office, print shop, and warehouse. Eight years ago she learned how to set type and now she has her own Chandler and Price letterpress in the room next to her kitchen "where housewives are supposed to have their washing machine" [36, p. 31]. Hejinian sets type the old-fashioned way, one letter at a time with a composing stick. Her first publication was a collection of her own poetry, but 26 of the 28 titles on her backlist are by other authors. Her average press run is 450 copies—50 for the author as payment, 250 for subscribers, and 150 for later orders.

The focus of this article has been the small book press, but it is important to remember that the role of the little magazine is crucial to that of the book press. Little magazines are often run by the same people who publish books, and in any case the talent that little magazines have traditionally discovered and encouraged often reaches a wider readership through book publication. Without the little magazine, many writers would never get their start. Well-known little magazines in this century were *Hound and Horn*, *Poetry* (still publishing in Chicago), *Furioso*, *Anvil*, and *Origin*. Some of the more important magazines publishing today are *Salmagundi*, *Chicago Review*, *Paris Review*, *Antaeus*, *Ploughshares*, *Southern Review*, *Kenyon Review*, *Raritan Review*, *Grand Street*, *Virginia Quarterly*, *Ontario Review*, *TriQuarterly*, and *Hudson Review*—to name but a few from a list that is almost endless. A good introduction to the world of contemporary little magazines is *The Little Magazine in*

America: A Modern Documentary History, edited by Elliott Anderson and Mary Kinzie [37].

Today's small book presses and little magazines are the result of a powerful movement that has swept torrents of people into publishing in the past two decades. While smaller publishers do not command the headlines that the conglomerates with their million-dollar deals and Hollywood tie-ins do, these thousands of smaller operations, through their spirit and their honesty of purpose, will probably mean far more to the future of American literary culture than the giants of Madison and Park Avenues.

REFERENCES

1. Henderson, Bill, ed. *The Pushcart Prize: Best of the Small Presses.* Yonkers, N.Y., and Wainscott, N.Y.: Pushcart Press, 1976–.
2. Fulton, Len, and Ferber, Ellen, eds. *International Directory of Little Magazines and Small Presses.* 18th ed. Paradise, Calif.: Dustbooks, 1982.
3. *Book Publishers Directory.* Detroit: Gale Research Co., 1977–.
4. Fulton, Len, and Ferber, Ellen, eds. *Small Press Record of Books in Print.* 11th ed. Paradise, Calif.: Dustbooks, 1982.
5. [Paine, Thomas.] *Common Sense: Addressed to the Inhabitants of America.* Philadelphia: R. Bell, 1776.
6. Henderson, Bill. "A Tradition of Do-It-Yourself Publishing." In *The Publish-It-Yourself Handbook.* Yonkers, N.Y.: Pushcart Press, 1973.
7. Knickerbocker, Diedrich [Washington Irving]. *A History of New York.* New York: Inskeep & Bradford, 1809.
8. Henderson, Bill. "Independent Publishing: Today and Yesterday." *Annals of the American Academy of Political and Social Science* 421 (September 1975): 93–105.
9. [Whitman, Walt.] *Leaves of Grass.* Brooklyn, N.Y., 1855.
10. Van Doren, Mark. "Whitman, Walt." In *Dictionary of American Biography,* edited by Dumas Malone. Vol. 20. New York: Charles Scribner's Sons, 1936.
11. [Whitman, Walt.] *Leaves of Grass.* Brooklyn, N.Y., 1856.
12. Whitman, Walt. *Leaves of Grass.* Boston: Thayer & Eldridge, 1860–61.
13. Whitman, Walt. *Leaves of Grass, with Sands at Seventy and A Backward Glance O'er Travel'd Roads . . . Portraits from Life.* Special ed. Philadelphia: Ferguson Bros. & Co., 1889.
14. Whitman, Walt. *Leaves of Grass, including Sands at Seventy, 1st Annex, Goodbye My Fancy, 2d Annex, A Backward Glance O'er Travel'd Roads, and Portrait from Life.* Philadelphia: D. McKay, [1892].
15. Twain, Mark [Samuel Langhorne Clemens]. *Adventures of Huckleberry Finn, Tom Sawyer's Comrade.* New York: Chas. L. Webster & Co., 1885.
16. Grant, Ulysses S. *Personal Memoirs of U. S. Grant.* New York: C. L. Webster & Co., 1885–86.
17. Sinclair, Upton. *The Jungle.* New York: Jungle Publishing Co., 1906.
18. Sinclair, Upton. *The Jungle.* New York: Doubleday, Page & Co., 1906.
19. Sandburg, Carl. *In Reckless Ecstasy.* Galesburg, Ill.: Asgard Press, 1904.
20. Nin, Anaïs. *The Winter of Artifice.* Paris: Obelisk Press, 1939.
21. Nin, Anaïs. *The Diary of Anaïs Nin.* Vol. 3. New York: Harcourt Brace Jovanovich, 1969.

22. Garson, Barbara. *MacBird*. Berkeley: Grassy Knoll Press, 1966.
23. Garson, Barbara. Conversation with the author. New York, September 1972.
24. Garson, Barbara. *MacBird*. New York: Grove Press, 1967.
25. Wigginton, Eliot, ed. *The Foxfire Book: Hog Dressing, Log Cabin Building, Mountain Crafts and Foods, Planting by the Signs, Snake Lore, Hunting Tales, Faith Healing, Moonshining, and Other Affairs of Plain Living.* Garden City, N.Y.: Anchor Press, 1972.
26. Wigginton, Eliot, ed. *Foxfire 2: Ghost Stories, Spring Wild Plant Foods, Spinning and Weaving, Midwifing, Burial Customs, Corn Shuckin's, Wagon Making and More Affairs of Plain Living.* Garden City, N.Y.: Anchor Press, 1973.
27. Wigginton, Eliot, ed. *Foxfire 3: Animal Care, Banjos and Dulcimers, Hide Tanning, Summer and Fall Wild Plant Foods, Butter Churns, Ginseng, and Still More Affairs of Plain Living.* Garden City, N.Y.: Anchor Press, 1975.
28. Wigginton, Eliot, ed. *Foxfire 4: Water Systems, Fiddle Making, Logging, Gardening, Sassafras Tea, Wood Carving, and Further Affairs of Plain Living.* Garden City, N.Y.: Anchor Press, 1977.
29. Wigginton, Eliot, ed. *Foxfire 5: Ironmaking, Blacksmithing, Flintlock Rifles, Bear Hunting, and Other Affairs of Plain Living.* Garden City, N.Y.: Anchor Press, 1979.
30. Wigginton, Eliot, ed. *Foxfire 6: Shoemaking, Gourd Banjos and Songbows, One Hundred Toys and Games, Wooden Locks, a Water Powered Sawmill, and Other Affairs of Just Plain Living.* Garden City, N.Y.: Anchor Press, 1980.
31. Gillespie, Paul F., ed. *Foxfire 7*. Garden City, N.Y.: Anchor Press, 1982.
32. Strachan, Bill, editor, Doubleday & Co. Conversation with the author, September 1974.
33. Spain, Hensley. *The Avocado Cookbook*. Berkeley: Creative Arts Book Co., 1979.
34. Ellis, Donald. "Up against Gulf + Western." *Publishers Weekly* 222 (September 10, 1982): 38–40.
35. Simon, Joan. "Permanence Is Paramount." *Publishers Weekly* 222 (September 10, 1982): 40.
36. Pine, Victoria. "For the Love of the Word." *Berkeley Monthly* 13 (December 1982): 27–31.
37. Anderson, Elliott, and Kinzie, Mary, eds. *The Little Magazine in America: A Modern Documentary History.* Yonkers, N.Y.: Pushcart Press, 1978.

THE PUBLISHING CULTURE AND THE LITERARY CULTURE

Ted Solotaroff[1]

The argument of this essay is that the traditional bridges between the literary culture and the publishing culture have increasingly weakened, if not begun to collapse, in the past decade or so. On the one hand, the publishing culture has become more and more like that of big business generally, marked by the broad effort to standardize the product, the distribution, and the consumer. Hence the increasing dominance of "brand-name authors" or categories and indeed of "lines" (like Silhouette, Harlequin, Executioner, etc.). Similarly, the advent of the bookstore chains put into practice the mass-merchandising system, and books began to be promoted as if they were merchandise no different from a bar of soap.

As the publishing culture moves away from its traditional commitments to standards of taste and to cultural responsibility, which the privately owned houses tended to exemplify, the literary culture appears to be becoming more and more elitist in its new home on the campuses. Most American writers today teach creative writing and/or literature, which significantly narrows the scope of their experience and awareness. At the same time, literary criticism is becoming more and more the province of the academic critics for whom structuralism and its offshoots are all the rage. Instead of stimulating and refining the tastes and interests of the prospective common readers of our society, literature in the academy today seems to be mainly the study of how the text is best served by having the critic supplant both the author and the common reader. Fortunately, however, many good books still make their way to the readers who relish and need them.

As a literary editor in a trade publishing house I lead a sort of double life. Much of my working days—and often most of my evenings and weekends—are spent with manuscripts of fiction, poetry, and intellectual prose that, more often than not, the industry that employs me regards as marginal and counterproductive until proved otherwise. Hence it is incumbent on me to foster this proof by doing what can be

1. Harper and Row Publishers, Inc., 10 East 53d Street, New York, New York 10022.

done to help these manuscripts become estimable and profitable. This means scrutinizing every sentence, responding to every point, suggesting any possible way the work can be made stronger, more interesting, more accessible, sometimes going through two or even three versions of a manuscript until it is as effective as the author can possibly make it. This also means playing an active role in the publishing process of distributing and marketing books by addressing its problems, talking its language, playing its game. The more unique a book is, the more one-of-a-kind, which are the only books I'm really interested in acquiring and working with, the less likely the industry is to know what to do with it or for it. In other words, if you want to be involved with such a book, you had better be prepared to chaperon it every step of the way and to create just the right aura for it in its physical appearance, its catalog and jacket copy, its words of welcome from other authors, its press release, which may help to get it reviewed, and its advertising copy, if you can manage to get any money to advertise it. In short, I am partly a practical critic who works more closely with a text than even a scholar does and partly a promoter of unlikely prospects, a bond salesman in an increasingly problematic market.

This partly explains why, between editing the *American Review* and the books I do, I have gone through four publishing houses in thirteen years. For during this period my double life has become more difficult, the split between the two cultures I work in more pronounced. Several major seismic developments have been separating these two archipelagos and making navigation between them more precarious. Put another way, as long as the literary culture and the publishing culture were adjacent to and facing each other, as they traditionally have been, they could reflect and implement each other's aspirations and needs, the pen yearning for the press, its public modality, as it were, the press, on the other hand, yearning for the fine pens that enabled it to move upward in society from a trade to a profession. By far, the most important development in trade publishing in recent times has been the transforming impact of the corporate mentality and methods as, one by one, the major publishing houses have been taken over by conglomerates or have become conglomerates themselves. At the same time, one by one, or rather ten by ten, the independent booksellers have been losing out to the giant marketing chains such as B. Dalton and Waldenbooks. Instigating and underwriting these developments has been the rapid expansion of the mass market for books, which, like any other mass market, operates by means of standardizing the product and the demand for it. The much-reported "blockbuster" phenomenon in book publishing can be viewed as the industry's effort to come as close as possible to producing and relying on brand-name products. So too the burgeoning "lines" of written-to-order romances and, lately, soft-core pornography that hog the racks in airports and drugstores.

These three interrelated forces work like pincers, narrowing the scope and prospects of literary and intellectual publishing. The publishing corporation, as distinct from the traditional publishing house, works, breathes, and wills like any other big business, at least at the management level. Its paramount concern is not the value of its product but the value of its shares which is keyed to its short-term profits, the number and profitability of books it sells rather than the quality of the books it sells. This tailoring of the product to the demand is more pronounced in paperback publishing, where the silent hand of the mass market is more coercive, but it inevitably affects hardcover publishing as well, both as the supplier of the reprinters and as a merchant looking for its piece of the action in the mass culture: that is, the books that service broad consumer needs or merely consumerism itself, that is, the need to keep buying or preparing or just wishing to buy that has turned the shopping mall into the church where so many Americans worship each weekend. This explains the shift, visible in most publishing houses, to consumer-oriented titles: the proliferation of cookbooks and diet books, self-help books, investment guides, crafts manuals, advice books on all stages of the life cycle.

Publishing for the shopping mall inevitably transforms the house that undertakes it by altering not only its procedures but also its functioning values; to borrow David Riesman's famous terms, it shifts these values from inner-directed to other-directed [1, pp. v–vi]. The traditional publishing house characteristically bore the name of its founder— Norton, Holt, Harper Brothers, Knopf, Morrow, Dutton, Farrar Straus, Simon and Schuster, and so forth—and developed along the lines of his vision, taste, and interests and those of his successors, who were chosen to maintain the house's established identity. Its functioning values tended to derive from a kind of idealized self-image of its founders, which, though adapted as it might be to later conditions and revised by subsequent directors, still maintained a remarkable continuity. The main reason for this was that the identity of the publishing house was protected from the fluctuations of taste and trend: profits were expected to be modest and variable given the nature of the business. Thus Alfred A. Knopf was free and able to develop a list of high international standing. Publishing for Knopf, a cultivated German Jew, was a means of joining his two cultural worlds at a high level, just as he personified this integration in his life-style and deportment. He is supposed to have said that he did not like to publish authors whom he would not like to invite to dinner.

One can trace much the same continuities through the other houses. For example, Harpers Brothers, for a century or more, bore the impress of its commitment as a book and magazine publisher to acting as an arbiter of American culture, particularly its political and social concerns. And, until fairly recently, it still tended to be the publisher of record, providing a forum for many important political figures and airing many important issues. Or again, publishers like James Laughlin and Barney Rosset, though they did not name their houses after themselves, still stamped their lists of authors with their own signatures. The scion of a steel fortune and a poet himself, Laughlin was the highest kind of patron, the one who supported his authors by publishing them, and he devoted New Directions mainly to discovering and disseminating the canon of the modern tradition in literature. Similarly, Rosset, an Irish Jew with a bohemian streak, made Grove Press into a kind of clearing house for the international avant-garde of the 1950s and 1960s. Though Laughlin and Rosset continue to publish, their houses are attenuated shadows of their former selves, leaving a large haunting absence in trade publishing of the risky, the experimental, the extreme literary work— the book that as often as not ushers in the future. This function has mainly passed to the small-press movement and increasingly to the university presses, where much of our innovative and difficult literature leads a dispersed and marginal existence.

Though Mr. Knopf has faded from the scene and his house has been owned by a series of conglomerates, it stands as one of the exceptions to the rule that such ownership leads to a dilution of identity, a loss of cultural mission, and a transformation of values by which the good but unusual book becomes marginal, and the bad, derivative book, in which, typically, a gimmick meets a fad, becomes highly commercial.

Why is this so? What happens when a conglomerate takes over a publishing house? Let us begin with a hypothetical example. Telcom, a far-flung media empire of newspapers, magazines, and television and radio stations, decides it wants the prestige and scope of owning a New York publishing house. It acquires Harbinger House, a venerable publisher of mostly quality books that has been hard hit by high interest rates, soaring manufacturing and overhead costs, and the depressed economy and badly needs the cash flow that Telcom is all too willing to supply. Then, in order to have both feet in the ring, as they say, Telcom buys Premium Books, a full-line paperback house, as well. For a time not much changes. The chief executive officer (CEO) of Telcom is content to let his new acquisitions run along in their accustomed and experienced ways. He has some fourteen subsidiaries under his wing and may find himself phoning room service in the morning to recall what city he is in. However, the profits of both houses remain flat in his terms: Harbinger around 7 percent, Premium around 12 percent, roughly one-half and two-thirds, respectively, of the overall profit levels of Telcom.

To "coordinate" his new trade-publishing operation, to fit it more symmetrically into Telcom's organizational chart, and to "goose" its management, the CEO sets up a new division and places it under the management of a Telcom executive who has no experience in publishing but was very successful in running the marketing division of Telcom's TV stations. This executive moves in with his team of financial and marketing analysts who quickly discover that trade publishing is a very irrational and uncertain way of doing business. For example, only 12 percent of Harbinger's list is responsible for 78 percent of its profits. Except for 2 titles, fiction books sell significantly less well than nonfiction books, and, of the latter, consumer-oriented books far exceed those of general interest, with the exception of biographies, though there it is necessary to distinguish between historical ones and celebrity ones. And so on and so forth. Title by title, category by category, editor by editor, the lists of both houses pass through the computer and produce the crystal-clear conclusion that the profit picture could be immediately and dramatically improved by publishing more books with a high return on investment and fewer books with a low one. Also, Premium's picture would be a lot rosier if it did not have to buy those expensive books from hardcover houses but rather from Harbinger and if it dropped all titles moving at a lower rate than a thousand a month and bought only those titles that could be expected to move at a higher rate. A Ludlum or a Carl Sagan comes high, but that is where the investment should be; acquiring James Michener and doing him in both editions is a license to print money; it is almost as exciting as picking off a competitive rival by a tender offer that cannot be refused.

What is likely to happen to the two houses' lists is obvious. At Harbinger, poetry is cut back to a few established authors; literary criticism pretty much departs, as does drama. Quality fiction comes under the marketing manager's scrutiny: Does it have a page-turning plot; sympathetic characters; a clear, lively, unfancy style; a topical subject; erotic interest? Is it, in short, a book that he himself likes to read? Collections of stories are highly dubious unless the author has been consistently published in the *New Yorker*. Each work of political and social criticism is similarly subjected to the standard of popular appeal: Is its point of view fashionable and palatable, immediately accessible, striking, controversial? Is its author, in short, likely to be invited to appear on the Phil Donahue Show? If not, is it likely to be adopted in college courses? So with psychology, biology, economics, religion. What is the market, and how do you reach it? All this has a subtle conditioning effect on even the more independent, venturesome, quality-minded editor. He finds that his value to the house has become quantified: his salary and overhead are now expected to produce x times their total in the net sales of the books he acquires. This pressure, as well as the changed atmosphere of the house itself, affects the way he reads, judges, and even edits manuscripts, his attention and influence imperceptibly but determinately shifting from the characteristics that make a book unique to those that make it marketable.

Fortunately, though, there are still countervailing winds that can help to keep him on his particular course. Even commercial-minded publishing does not lend itself all that readily to the kind of controls that corporate managers like to employ to tailor the product to the market. The reading tastes and interests of the book-buying public still tend to be more individualized than any computer can track. Once you get past the proven best-selling authors and the trashier categories and lines of pop writing, you are in a gray area of crude comparisons, hunches, and surprises. Also, American book publishing still operates in a very big and diverse country that has been educating a lot of people. That is why even the beleaguered editor at Harbinger House remains haunted by the tutelary spirit of art and ideas. For the literary or intellectual work that strikes it rich can strike it very rich indeed, and for years to come. First novels may generally lose money, but how would you like to have passed up *Catcher in the Rye, Catch-22, The Naked and the Dead,* or *Invisible Man*? A writer whose first four novels did not sell is hard to justify to the salesforce and bookstore buyer, but how would you like to have turned down *The World according to Garp, The Adventures of Augie March,* or *The French Lieutenant's Woman*? So all but the most shortsighted editors and publishers tend to maintain a margin of imagination and venture capital for at least a few of those strange, disturbing manuscripts that do not fit in anywhere but may turn out to have been written by the next Tom Robbins or Sylvia Plath.

Nonetheless, the current marketplace makes it more difficult to establish the one-of-a-kind book, for the pressures I have been indicating that operate in the publishing houses are even more onerous at the other end of the process. Two major developments in bookselling are at work here. The first is the spectacular growth of the bookstore chains, such as B. Dalton and Waldenbooks, which control about 20 percent of the market and deeply influence the rest of it. A recent article in *Publishers Weekly* carried the following description of the Waldenbooks mentality: "All [of its top executives] strongly support the mass merchandising concept (that is, of treating books like a product in the same way a manufacturer would merchandise a bar of soap). Hoffman [the president], who views romance titles with as much respect as literary works, experienced the selling power of mass merchandising techniques when he was an executive at Bell & Howell . . ." [2, p. 37]. The way profitability is reckoned at Walden and Dalton is quite literally on a "sales per square foot basis." This means that a book will be ordered or not on the basis of its sales predictability and will remain in the store or not on the basis of its sales performance, in which it competes with every other book in the store as either a frontlist (recently published) or a backlist item. The acceptable rates of sale are fed into a central computer, and if a book does not quickly meet them, it is replaced. The book by a relatively unknown author that does not have a substantial first printing and advertising budget either does not get into the chain bookstores at all or its few nominal copies are lost in the shuffle of the best-sellers and the traffic of the category consumer books.

An even more ominous phenomenon is the advent of the discount bookstore chains, such as Crown Books and Barnes and Noble, that narrow the market even further by restricting their inventories to current books that have a rapid turnover and books being remaindered. The main trouble with both kinds of chains is not that they exist (no one in publishing is opposed to selling as many books as possible) but that they make it increasingly difficult for the independent bookseller to survive unless he turns his store into the same kind of high-volume discount operation as the chains. This is a serious loss for quality publishing because the independent bookseller provided the specialized advice and service to readers, including a congenial atmosphere for browsing, that gave the one-of-a-kind book the chance to reach its limited but nonetheless dependable audience. As an outpost as well as conduit of the literate culture in most communities, the endangered and indeed vanishing condition of the independent bookseller vitiates the principal alternative to the mass merchandising of books and its distorting and withering consequences and implications for the publishing culture. As one of my colleagues puts it, quoting a poet you are unlikely to find in any shopping mall, "The best lack all conviction, while the worst / Are full of passionate intensity" [3, p. 215].

I began by speaking of the widening gulf between the publishing culture and the literary or even literate one. For if the former is advancing steadily into the mass culture, the latter is retreating to a significant extent from it into the confines of the university. I have noted that an increasing amount of literary and intellectual publishing is being taken on by the university presses. At the same time, most of our novelists, poets, and critics depend on teaching as their principal livelihood, as do our more significant writers in most other fields. One can say that this is all to the good in that it has solved the age-old problem of how serious writers are to live, particularly in a society where one has to earn fifteen thousand dollars a year just to survive—about three times the average earnings of published writers.

One way this has been accomplished is by developing programs in creative writing. In 1952 when I was looking for a writing program there were exactly two to choose from: Iowa and Stanford. Today, at last count, there are close to 500 schools that grant B.A.'s and M.F.A.'s in writing, and their numbers increase every year because they are very popular. Indeed, formerly the tail of an English department, the writing program now tends to wag the dog. The course in writing lyric poetry is oversubscribed, while the course in the Elizabethan lyric has been dropped because only a handful of students were signing up for it. When I asked a friend of mine who teaches fiction writing at a Texas university what his students were writing, he glumly replied, "Mostly imitations of Star Trek." The proliferation of writing students seems to me partly a function of our much-noticed age of narcissism and partly a function of the shrinkage of distance between the writer and the consumer that is fostered by the mass market. But even the gifted young writer, the one with a future, may well find himself on a track that leads from a writing major, to one of the graduate workshops, and on to a position of teaching writing himself. This means that what he increasingly knows most about is campus life, which means that most sectors of specific public experience are closed off to him. One can chart in many if not most of the oeuvres of our leading fiction writers a movement from a concern with the people and piece of the world they came out of to either a preoccupation with the university ambiance and their life within it or else a preoccupation with some master fantasy or simply with innovations in technique. The marketing manager who says to me, "Who wants to read another novel about a professor who is screwing a student and fighting with his colleagues?" has a point. Or another apocalyptic, black-humor novel, or another collection of plotless stories with characterless characters. Also one can see in the regnant school of academic criticism, structuralism/deconstructionism, a further stage in what Ortega y Gasset termed "the dehumanization" of literature [4], one that removes even the author from the text by disconnecting his circuitry of meaning and thereby gives the text an independent, arbitrary, and hermetic existence waiting to be inhabited by the critic. None of this seems to me very useful for a viable and significant literary culture. Meanwhile the perplexing, ominous, distressed common life of our society goes on: real people coping with bewildering changes. Amid the steady stream of escapist trash, proliferating from year to year, one looks for the literary works that have some sense of necessity in them, that can matter to readers because they help them to understand their lives and to bear them better.

I recently published at Harper and Row a collection of short stories called *Shiloh,* a first book by a forty-year-old writer named Bobbie Ann Mason [5]: no advertising or publicity and a distribution of 2,200 copies, which meant that roughly one out of three bookstores had a copy of it.

But despite all of the adverse circumstances that I have been charting and grousing about, the book began to catch on. The stories deal mostly with contemporary women and their families in small towns in western Kentucky who find that they have slipped the moorings of the traditional rural folkways and are trying to figure out where to turn next. All across the country, in the cities and towns and campuses, reviews turned up—not so much reviews as hands raised in welcome and recognition. These wry, sad, respectful stories are now in their fifth printing. And much the same success, for many of the same reasons, is about to descend upon a Chicago writer named Joan Chase, whose first novel, *During the Reign of the Queen of Persia* [6], is also a one-of-a-kind book on a theme pressing for expression: the rivalries and bondings among three generations of women on a farm in Ohio. It is no accident that both books are by mature women, for women writers today have a genuine subject and a passionate constituency, and a really gifted writer—an Alice Walker, Alice Munro, or Anne Tyler, a Lynne Schwartz or a Marilynne Robinson—is able to surmount the obstacles that the conglomerates and the bookstore chains and the mass culture itself place between her and her readers. So what it comes down to, I guess, is that editors like myself can only insist and persist so much; we need the right books, those that speak forcefully to our private imaginations and public concerns, for only they can join once again the literary culture and the publishing culture, if only here and there, and keep the two from being pulled completely asunder.

REFERENCES

1. Riesman, David. "Preface." In *The Lonely Crowd: A Study of the Changing American Character,* by David Riesman in collaboration with Reuel Denny and Nathan Glazer. New Haven, Conn.: Yale University Press, 1950.
2. Frank, Jerome B. "Waldenbooks at Fifty." *Publishers Weekly* 223 (April 29, 1983): 36–41.
3. Yeats, William Butler. "The Second Coming." In *The Collected Poems of W. B. Yeats.* New York: Macmillan Publishing Co., 1934.
4. Ortega y Gasset, José. *The Dehumanization of Art, and Notes on the Novel.* Princeton, N.J.: Princeton University Press, 1948.
5. Mason, Bobbie Ann. *Shiloh and Other Stories.* New York: Harper & Row, 1982.
6. Chase, Joan. *During the Reign of the Queen of Persia.* New York: Harper & Row, 1983.

ISSUES OF STRUCTURE AND CONTROL IN THE SCHOLARLY COMMUNICATION SYSTEM

Charles B. Osburn[1]

This article begins with the identification of the library perception of forces out of control in the scholarly communication system and proceeds to a description of attempts libraries are making to regain a sense of control. In reaction to papers prepared by publishers, the article then addresses points of similarity or contrast between scholarly publishers and research libraries, with emphasis on the concept of selectivity. Possibilities for the restructuring and control of certain aspects of the scholarly communication system are suggested.

Introduction

The perspective on scholarly publishing that I have been asked to represent is that of a university library director with special interests in collection development. Most likely I was given this assignment because my collection development experience in five universities suggests a sound basis for expertise. But the truth of the matter is that this experience has provided a solid basis only for confusion. As a preface to this paper I want to make it clear that the views expressed are mine only, and that they do not necessarily represent the views of any constituency. I also want to announce, in response to Morris Philipson's interpretation of the relationship between librarians and publishers [1], that I have never held an attitude of antagonism toward publishers. I understand and am very sympathetic toward the publisher's conflict between intrinsic value and market value, for it lies at the heart of collection development decisions in an academic research library.

The term "collection development" is not library jargon, but it is used in the library profession to define a function peculiar to that profession which perhaps should be explained in this forum. Collection develop-

1. University of Cincinnati Libraries, Cincinnati, Ohio 45221.

ment is the process of decision making that determines how the library's resources supporting research and instruction should develop: which books, journals, and other materials should be part of the library's resources and which should not. Frederick Praeger observes: "The publisher is the quality-control center of the scholarly information business" [2, p. 24]. Similarly, collection development sorts through the universe of publications generated through publishers' manuscript selection and distribution and applies its own selection criteria derived from a local university's mission and goals. There is an obvious inherent dependency of the collection development process on the processes expected of the publisher. Lewis Coser identifies an even greater role for the publisher, depending on judgment and courage, in his statement: "It is only if and when they [publishers] are able to buck trends, at least for a significant number of the books they publish, that they assume full stature as molders of culture" [3, p. 12]. Libraries, as further disseminators and as preservers of publishers' contributions to the molding of culture, may also be evaluated on this basis. But for research libraries there is a serious conflict because reflecting cultural trends, in an archival sense, is one of the essential roles of research libraries.

Recently, the fundamental issue of intrinsic value versus market value, which corresponds in library collection development to the issue of collection building versus service, has become extraordinarily ambiguous. It has been rendered ambiguous from the library perspective, and one can infer also from the publishing perspective, because of a growing conviction in library circles that cooperation offers a partial solution to the array of impediments to fulfillment of the mission and because of the growing evidence that technology can facilitate the realization of plans to cooperate regionally and nationally in the provision of information resources to scholarship. If publishers feel uncertain about the future, and even about the present, librarians are equally uncertain and concerned. Some forces in our respective environments seem to be out of control.

Forces out of Control

A sufficient number of charts, graphs, tables, and laments have been published in recent years demonstrating the rapid escalation in prices of books and journals; from them you know immediately that price inflation constitutes one of the great forces out of control from the library perspective. There is nothing I can add to that picture overall. But I do want to point out another trend within that framework: the growing importance the journal, as opposed to the book, has developed in academic research libraries.

As the library traditionally has been the heart of the university, so has the collection been the center of academic research library attention. Protection of the materials budget—the book budget, as it often is called—has therefore always been a high priority. Even though technology is adding new costs in libraries and even though library staff are under an ever-increasing workload, somehow academic research libraries, represented by the median statistics of member institutions in the Association of Research Libraries (ARL), showed a rather consistent and stable commitment to the book budget between 1975 and 1982 (see table 1), which was a fairly difficult time for library financing. Whether or not this was always a wise choice in the long term is a question we need not address here, but the point is that only through great effort and, probably, sacrifice could a steady, high percentage of the total operating budgets of research libraries be maintained for materials. This has been generally at the 30 percent level. At the same time, the number of journal subscriptions increased by about 10 percent, while the dollar value of those subscriptions more than doubled. As a consequence of this trend, the percentage of the median ARL library materials budget spent on journals climbed from about 45 percent to nearly 60 percent, and I do not see evidence of this trend's changing. When you consider the implications of subscription rather than item purchase, it is a situation that seems to be out of control, even though, in theory, we librarians have the authority to control it. (Parenthetically, the question of authority, responsibility, and accountability of the library in the university would be an interesting study in its own right.)

The growing importance of journals to scholarship, that is, the process that causes this change in value, is another force over which the library perceives itself as having no control and that seems to be evolving out of control. This process is constituted by three major elements. One is the constantly changing set of methodologies and goals of research, another is the snowballing nature of research, and a third is the whole academic ethos that is affected profoundly by the first two. I can refer to these phenomena only most superficially in this paper, but the point is that librarians can do little more than react to and accommodate these changes, if they even are alert enough to know about them.

Academic research libraries have evolved from being book-centered agencies to more journal- or serial-oriented agencies. And now we may begin to see the potential of a further shift toward a technology-based agency. This raises the question of the impact of technology in academic research libraries, and technology is one of those forces that I would describe as developing out of control, from the viewpoint of a librarian, at least. Of course, we do not control technological development. But, to the extent that user expectations for library and information services are

TABLE 1

THE CONSTRICTING PARAMETERS OF DECISION MAKING IN ACADEMIC RESEARCH LIBRARY COLLECTION DEVELOPMENT

Fiscal Year	Subscriptions (N)	Subscription Expenditures ($)	Subscriptions as % of Total Materials Expenditures	Total Materials Expenditures ($)	Materials as % of Total Operating Expenditures	Total Operating Expenditures ($)
1981–82	20,054	1,107,499	56.3	1,966,439	32.5	6,047,575
1980–81	19,378	1,059,653	59.4	1,783,144	34.1	5,232,703
1979–80	19,568	904,190	55.2	1,637,405	34.2	4,783,864
1978–79	18,909	825,121	53.2	1,550,206	33.7	4,605,041
1977–78	19,146	713,139	50.9	1,400,931	31.4	4,467,578
1976–77	18,511	590,745	46.0	1,285,131	33.3	3,863,299
1975–76	18,876	526,594	44.9	1,173,503	33.6	3,490,754

SOURCE.—[4].
NOTE.—Figures used represent the median of reporting libraries.

raised by an awareness of the potential applications of technology, we are stimulated from all sides to make use of it, perhaps sooner than our organization and whole social environment can cope with it properly. Moreover, it is clear that technology, through its potential for publication, transmission, storage, and retrieval of texts as well as data and other images, is creating a whole new range of formats for information and knowledge. For libraries, this translates into a new, and as yet undefined, concept of collection. I think that this relates to Frederick Praeger's observation about technology blurring the distinctions between scholar, publisher, and librarian [2, pp. 21–22].

Even without the new electronic formats the universe of publication and information seems to grow uncontrollably from the librarian's standpoint. Just think of the number of books, journals, reports, government documents, and microforms generated each year. Then think of the desperate concern we have about the preservation of materials already acquired and already deteriorating. Then think of the declining purchasing power of higher education and the evidently diminishing willingness of private donors to support university libraries. Budgets, staffs, abilities, and energies seem inadequate to meet demand, at least on an institution-by-institution basis.

So we in academic research library collection development are very concerned when we perceive that the traditional editorial functions of the publisher either are being abdicated by some publishers who do not wish to bear those costs or are being circumvented as a result of facile creation and distribution made possible by computer technology. We are troubled by a massive movement of small presses, not because we are opposed to free enterprise or American literature, but because it simply becomes much more difficult to distinguish the significant and the excellent from the other works of fiction. The point in both cases is that we depend very heavily on the judgment of the publisher in selecting manuscripts for publication. Over the years we get to know which publishers are doing a good job and are trustworthy, and we can base selection partly on their record. But when a peer review process for manuscript selection is discontinued, or federal funds make possible a great number of new publishers whose work has the physical appearance of quality yet who cannot necessarily be counted on to select manuscripts carefully, then we feel that the situation is unstructured and out of control.

Control Measures of Academic Research Libraries

Not content with the role of merely responding in this ambiguous, changing, and problematic situation, academic research libraries are engaged in several efforts to establish order for their purposes. Fore-most is the national trend toward reconsidering the concept of selectivity and the various ways that concept is brought to bear on the development of collections in this changing environment. That this trend was generated by the declining purchasing power of the budget for current book and journal acquisitions seems certain. But the growing spectrum of resources, sources, and services providing information of all kinds via electronic media undoubtedly is going to require continued redefinition of the concept of selectivity because it begins to influence our essential understanding of the word "collections" in the context of library support for academic research. As the proportion of the knowledge and information universe traditionally occupied by books gradually is displaced by electronic media of all kinds, what does the word "collection" really mean, and how does that relate to the concept of selectivity in collection development? These are questions academic research librarians are attempting to answer as one measure of control in a complex environment.

In that connection, Frederick Praeger describes some of these increasing complexities in the scholarly communications system, fearing that easy self-publication through electronic means is, alone, a new force with which librarians must cope, and one with which we may not cope well, to the detriment of traditional scholarly publishing [2]. Without being able to allay those fears entirely, I do want to suggest that only the quantity of publications involved will be different for us, not the principle of self-publication. I am referring to the similarity, from the library perspective, between the potential of easy and automatic publishing of the future and traditional vanity press publishing. But, again, our capacity to deal selectively with automatic electronic self-publishing will be determined just as our capacity to deal selectively with vanity press publications has been. We will select on the basis of our knowledge that some scholarly and commercial publishers do apply criteria of quality to their selection of publishable communication before those publications come to our attention.

A significant benefit of academic research librarians' determining criteria for selection is the communication and collaboration between library and faculty that it requires. It is my belief that academic research libraries have developed in the past three decades too independently of the community they were intended to serve—at least insofar as collection development is concerned. But now this is changing for the better. We are beginning to structure two-way communication through the evaluation and review of collections, through the establishment of formal and comprehensive policy on the development of collections, through the establishment of approval plan profiles with book vendors, through the development of methodology for the allocation of acquisition funds, and through the screening of recommended new subscriptions and expensive single purchases. "Collection development," as a term describing a function, is being replaced in our vocabulary by the term "collection management," which more accurately expresses a new emphasis in the function, manifested by the activities just itemized, as well as by a heightened concern for the relationship between dollars available and service required.

From the publisher's point of view, I imagine that the most significant example of a new emphasis on good management in direct support of service to scholarship nationally is the movement toward networking and resource sharing. This is something that has been discussed a great deal within the profession for many decades, albeit with little action following from that discussion. However, now we are confronted with the reality that each library can no longer attempt to operate independently of others and hope to provide good service to scholarship. At the same time, technology offers the promise of successful cooperative ventures. Bill Henderson reminds us of the important function of small presses in American literary history, noting that "the unique importance of today's small presses . . . [is] the preservation and advancement of creative literature" [5, p. 61]. Few would challenge this view, and many would no doubt feel strongly that a good representation of contemporary American literary history—the primary sources—ought to be found in American university libraries. But how can this be? How can we all possibly afford the books, the staff, and the space to accomplish this, each library with its own resources, independently? We cannot. And this, of course, is the fundamental reason for cooperation among academic research libraries. We want to be sure that within a library network of support to scholarship nationwide these books are acquired in sufficient number, preserved, and made accessible to scholars throughout the nation. Please note well that we will not save money by doing this. We will spend more. What we will accomplish is better service in both the short and long term. Collectively, we will buy books and journals that we would not otherwise buy independently.

Perceptions and Practices

Based on the papers presented at this conference, it is my estimation that there are far more similarities between publishers and librarians in the scholarly communication system than there are differences. However, there probably are some misperceptions from both vantage points, and doubtless there are some true differences. Lewis Coser, who has de-

scribed clearly the major distinguishing sociological features of the publishing industry, offers us an excellent framework in which to apply
comparisons between that industry and the academic research library
business. For example, Coser's observations about the diversity of size,
operating procedures, and relations to the market apply quite well to the
academic research libraries of North America. When he refers to the
"golden days of the past when personal criteria, individual taste, and a
sense of cultural responsibility governed decisions" [3, p. 6], the librarian is reminded of the shift from collection development to collection management in research libraries. A very provocative distinction
drawn between the automobile industry and the publishing industry,
emphasizing the high degree of standardized procedures and the great
extent to which major decisions are made at the top of the organization
in the automobile industry [3, pp. 6–7], underscores the similarities between scholarly publishing and librarianship. It is most instructive to
bear in mind Coser's assessment that the publishing industry "hardly
conducts any market research" [3, p. 7], for when we consider that
academic research libraries do not either, it becomes evident that there is
a compounded problem in the scholarly communication system. During
the past few decades research library collection development has been
directed by intuition rather than by knowledge of the market. The Coser
paper suggests other analogies between the two enterprises, but I will
mention only one.

There is a fundamental distinction between publishing and other
industries that summarizes very well the essence of similarity between
publishing and librarianship in the scholarly communication system.
Coser remarks: "To the extent that the publishing industry attempts to
operate like any other industry it fails to live up to its cultural responsibilities" [3, p. 9]. He goes on to discuss the perilous position of
publishing, situated between the demands of commerce and the demands of culture. This, of course, is the intrinsic versus market value
issue, raised in a different way, and it expresses very well the conflict in
research library collection development between building collections of
absolute value and managing collections as a service. While every book
need not turn a profit to the scholarly publisher, it is still also true that
every book need not circulate frequently and widely in a research library. We have our eighty-twenty rule. I do not know what publishers
have. Causing the balance to shift one way and the other in both enterprises are the diverse publics we serve and the many lines of accountability with which both must cope. Publishers are accountable to stockholders, investors, the educated public, the common reader, and the
community of intellectuals and scholars, according to Lewis Coser [3].
Academic research libraries are accountable to faculty, students, librari-

ans, administration, other libraries in the region, and the broader scholarly community. And within this group I can assure you that the criteria are not just mixed, but often in conflict.

Rita Lerner notes that publishers are trying to gain control over production costs and, consequently, over publication prices to the consumer by applying computer technology to composition [6, p. 42]. We librarians applaud this, I believe, and reply that, for our part, we are trying to preserve our acquisitions budgets by applying computer technology to the processing functions of the library. Yet in other areas of the library, computer expenditures are new and rising, for the computer and related technology open vast new service possibilities that we simply must make available to our communities. Cost containment may be realized in processing, but the overall enterprise of the academic research library very naturally is evolving toward much greater expense, most of it driven upward by technology.

This brings us to a complaint lodged by Frederick Praeger, who finds that a major problem confronting the publishing industry results directly from the general public belief that information and knowledge should be free [2, p. 24]. Clearly, this is a problem not just for publishing but equally for libraries and for the whole scholarly communication system. In research libraries, we have not established a good precedent for cost recovery of information services, of which we offer an increasingly broad range. Now, however, we must consider inaugurating and expanding costs in an environment that is not going to be conducive to this movement. This is especially crucial now since many more of these information services are assuming the characteristics of a utility and as the cost of personnel time, always in greater demand, increases with the ever-rising qualifications of information personnel. I believe these concerns are similar to some of the real world elements Morris Philipson associates with the publishing industry [1].

Areas of Conflict

Publishers and librarians in the scholarly communication system seem to experience conflict in five areas, all of which are intertwined, of course. First, there is the intrinsic value versus market value conflict that affects both agents in the system. Although this conflict presents us with difficult and costly decisions, the right choices do determine the extent to which either agent is of value to society. In that regard, we should be glad that there is, indeed, such a conflict, and we should strive to guarantee that the conflict continues and is not driven out by popular demand or by the economy of effort. Would you consider me too naive and romantic if I were to suggest that choice is what distinguishes humans from other animals and that the more altruistic and abstract the choice the greater the distinction? Would you agree that the degree of involvement in and exercise of this kind of choice separates the leaders from the followers, the great from the lesser, and the potential from the limit?

Then there is the conflict that arises because of the essentially competitive nature of the publishing industry and the increasingly cooperative nature of research libraries. It is not clear to me whether publishers are more competitive about manuscript acquisition or about market growth, or whether that makes any difference. Whatever the case may be, it is evident that publishers are worried about the diminishment of competitive spirit among research libraries. Both areas need to be understood better than they are.

Third on my list of conflicts is the role of technology. The question is, Is technology a solution to the problems of the scholarly communication system or is it another mounting problem? It probably is both; but we need to understand the potential of technology from both perspectives and then do our best to increase the solution potential and decrease the problem potential.

Then there is a conflict that arises because of the management introspection of both the publishing industry and research librarianship. Publishers are mightily concerned about profit and market viability—as they must be—while academic research librarians are equally concerned about efficiency of operations—as they must be. However, being shortchanged in these traumas is the remaining part of the scholarly communication system—the scholars. Frederick Praeger says that librarians "focus exclusively on the consumer, on providing rapid access to information already on hand" [2, p. 28]. I take comfort in that thought and am pleased if it looks that way from outside. But I am more convinced that we have not focused so much on the consumer's goals, methods, habits, and motivations as we have on the efficiency of techniques to control and retrieve to our own professional satisfaction. This may just be a question of emphasis and the end results of either emphasis could possibly be quite similar. But Praeger is right, in my estimation, that by and large we have not focused our attention on the scholarly communication system, the "exchange system of idea and thought" [2, p. 28]. I submit that publishers have behaved similarly.

Finally, there are the conflicts that arise because of erroneous assumptions and misperceptions adopted by both agents in the scholarly communication system. In one way or another the papers presented here have brought these to mind. And that most certainly is good because this source of conflict will have to be addressed before further progress can be made toward control and structuring of the system in the best interest of society.

Conclusions toward an Agenda

It may be arrogant, bordering on the preposterous, for me to suggest an agenda for the improvement of our contributions to the scholarly communication system, but an agenda can be inferred from discussions of the past two days. Indeed this conference is an item on the long-term agenda, as was the Wingspread conference on research libraries, held in December 1982, which included publishers and scholars as well as foundation representatives. What I wish to do in concluding these remarks is to pose a few questions for the publishers, list some issues that we could address jointly to our mutual benefit, and suggest that we collaborate where we can do so productively in areas of common concern, while striving to understand where our true differences lie.

One reservation before proceeding: I am very much in favor of collaboration but have reservations about collaboration in all ways. For example, libraries are not consumers of publishers' products and should not behave or be considered as such. We would want to be sure that publishers and librarians do not work out common determiners of the kinds of books and journals for which there is a ready market. This would apply artificial controls to the system that could render operations orderly for librarians and publishers but would introduce a strange kind of censorship. Librarians should not collaborate with publishers by attempting to describe market needs other than in the most general terms.

Before noting some of the areas in which I think collaboration could be most fruitful, here are, for the record, a few questions for the publishers, some of which may have no answers:

1. Earlier I referred to the eighty-twenty rule in research libraries, which suggests that 80 percent of use of books and journals is provided by 20 percent of the collection. (The 20 percent is elusive, thereby helping us rationalize our mistakes in selection.) This is similar to the commerce versus culture or intrinsic value versus market value conflicts in publishing, for a good research library is expected to have little-used materials that are significant to the intellectual integrity of the collection. The question is, Could the scholarly publishing industry develop a guideline similar to this so-called eighty-twenty rule to ensure the publication of those important, but low-demand, books and journals? Can this be structured?

2. If some publishers of journals can levy page charges to authors and also raise subscription prices to libraries and others, what other forces help control selection of manuscripts?

3. Different formats of publication serve different purposes in different fields. There are prestige values, requirements to communicate broadly but rapidly, archival or historical record purposes, and others. Can the publishing industry structure this better so that the format conforms more closely with anticipated consumption by the market?

4. Can the duplication of publication be reduced, especially in science and technology journals, thus controlling the volume and complexity of the bibliographic universe?

5. Rita Lerner informs us that at least in one scientific area journal subscriptions seem to be dropping by about 2 percent annually [6, p. 41]. Yet the number of library subscriptions grows at about 2 percent annually and the expenditure at a much greater rate. To what extent could consolidation of fields, rather than a splintering of fields, along with greater selectivity in manuscript selection, alter this unfortunate trend?

In terms of areas where collaboration between scholarly publishers and research librarians could be fruitful, the following is a list, in no order of priority, of some of the more evident possibilities.

1. While Rita Lerner observes that through technology, single-article distribution challenges the viability of the publication system [6, p. 44], Peter Urbach expresses confidence that technology really will solve many of the major problems separating librarians and publishers [7, p. 32]. Technology seems to be an area of unknown. Working with scholars, the two enterprises should monitor and give guidance jointly to the development of communication technology as it influences the scholarly communication system.

2. Frederick Praeger advises us to arrive at new definitions "in concert rather than each in his own semi-isolated discipline" [2, p. 28]. I suggest that we take his advice and begin very specifically by defining, in concert with scholars, the scholarly communication system—its motives, its parts, its patterns, and its parameters.

3. We could monitor jointly trends in scholarly communication, noting problems, opportunities, areas for development.

4. We really should monitor jointly, advise on, and take action on national policy that does have or could be made to have an impact on the scholarly communication system.

5. We could very productively advise on relevant professional education and training programs.

6. To one extent or another we are all struggling to comprehend the meaning and implications of a so-called information society. But I be-

lieve we will slip quietly through that phase and move toward a society that values not just information but, even more important, knowledge. We could begin to discuss the potential and implications of this kind of evolution and our likely role in it.

7. We could collaborate on a systematic, organized program to help the public understand the legitimate costs of information and knowledge.

8. Relating matters of national policy to the question of cost of information and knowledge, we could, in the best interests of society, experiment with structures for the funding of a scholarly communication system that operates in a more sophisticated manner than by simply passing charges along directly to the consumer who is able to pay.

9. We can continue to collaborate on technical matters, such as the quality of paper, print, and binding, and on the determination of most apropriate format for distribution.

There must be many other areas quite suitable for concerted efforts among publishers, librarians, and scholars, and I know that the areas just itemized are not going entirely unattended. But I should hope that the present conference really is another item on the national agenda that will lead to the establishment of a forum to address these matters integrally and consistently. As has been suggested by others, the time seems ripe for us to look outward from our specific, internal preoccupations and consider the realization of a larger system in the service of society.

REFERENCES

1. Philipson, Morris. "Intrinsic Value versus Market Value." In this issue.
2. Praeger, Frederick A. "Librarians, Publishers, and Scholars, Common Interests, Different Views: The View of an Independent Scholarly Publisher." In this issue.
3. Coser, Lewis A. "The Publishing Industry as a Hybrid." In this issue.
4. Association of Research Libraries. *ARL Statistics.* Washington, D.C.: Association of Research Libraries, 1976–82.
5. Henderson, Bill. "The Small Book Press: A Cultural Essential." In this issue.
6. Lerner, Rita G. "The Professional Society in a Changing World." In this issue.
7. Urbach, Peter F. "The View of a For-Profit Scientific Publisher." In this issue.

THE FOUNDATION FOR THE DIALOGUE

Lester Asheim[1]

Publishers and librarians both serve as gatekeepers of ideas and guardians of the written culture. They are subject to the same social forces that shape that culture and are equally sensitive to both the promise and the threat of the New Technology. What sets them apart is, primarily, the commercial considerations that directly affect the publishers' gatekeeper role but only indirectly affect that of the librarians. This does not mean that economic forces do not affect the librarian; rising costs are felt by both publisher and librarian, and, particularly for the librarian, the present probability that services once offered without charge may soon be available only for a fee creates a real conflict with the "free" public library idea and the traditional librarian's belief in everyone's right to have access to needed information. If the term "support" is substituted for the idea of "profit," however, the distinction between the publisher and the librarian becomes less great. Both must come to terms with the New Technology and still try to retain the best in both the publishing and library traditions. It is in this context of mutual commitment to the service of society that the publisher/librarian dialogue should be carried out.

The question which faces this conference seems to me to be not whether there is a foundation for dialogue between publishers and librarians but, rather, Why should such closely associated partners in the communication enterprise feel the need to raise the question at all? How can publishers and librarians not engage in the kind of dialogue that this conference proposes—and exemplifies? Do we not have much more in common than there are forces that keep us apart?

Look, for example, at the definition of the publisher's role, suggested by Coser and his colleagues, and frequently cited in this conference, as that of a gatekeeper of ideas and guardian of our written culture [1, p. 362]. Surely that is a description that applies to librarians as well, and if the publisher is one-up on librarians as the "constant creator" of a major carrier of those ideas and that culture, the librarian plays a more readily

1. University of North Carolina at Chapel Hill, School of Library Science, 100 Manning Hall 026-A, Chapel Hill, North Carolina 27514.

94

identifiable role as the preserver and retriever of those carriers. Together we form a mutually supportive role in the total function of making ideas available.

Coser et al. suggest another aim of the publisher: "To get the message to the right people" [1, p. 200]. Compare that formulation with the aim of librarianship as enunciated by Francis Drury in 1930: "To provide the right book for the right reader at the right time" [2, p. 1]. We have shared the very words of our mutual aim for over half a century. The correlation of the goals of publishing and librarianship is one of long standing.

Note also how sensitive we both must be to the social forces that affect the written culture. I turn again to Coser and his colleagues for their identification of the influences that affect book publishing: "Book publishing has changed in the past two decades. It has been affected by societal trends, including a real growth in literacy, the increased number of college graduates, the expansion of the higher educational system, a worldwide information explosion, and an enormous boom in the mass entertainment industry" [1, p. 25]. Even if we were to add to that statement the latest developments, or even unreached potentialities, of the New Technology that occupied so many of our discussions, we could still substitute the word "librarianship" for "book publishing" and not have to change another word to keep it an accurate description. Thus, since we serve the same goals and are affected by the same social forces, we are, as the saying goes, all in this thing together.

Which means, of course, that we are also dependent on each other to a large degree. I will readily admit that librarians probably are more dependent on publishers than they are on us. It would seem obvious enough that if all book publishing should come to a halt, libraries as we now conceive them would soon have little function other than that of preserving a historical artifact for archival purposes. Still, it should be remembered that there were "libraries" before there were "books" in the sense that we use those terms today, and that libraries—or at least the social function served by libraries—will still need to be carried out by some formal mechanism, no matter what medium becomes the prime carrier of ideas.

On the other hand, if all libraries should disappear tomorrow, book publishing could still go on, but it could not go on in quite the same manner. "A sizable portion of the industry's output goes to a host of libraries and then reaches the public . . ." [1, p. 337], according to the Coser volume; and the decline in library budgets has been cited by several of the speakers as a major challenge for publishers—an acknowledgment of the library's place in the market considerations of at least some segments of the publishing world.

As gatekeepers and guardians, publishers and librarians have stood together against onslaughts of those who would censor, repress, lock up, or destroy the word—not only in print but in any format that carries a message which some segments of the population would suppress if they could. When faced with that common enemy—the fear of the word—we have joined forces with great effectiveness and have recognized that here eternal vigilance and mutual support will continue to be required of us. As Henderson's paper pointed out [3], in every period and in every literature there have been rejected works which have come later to be recognized and valued because somehow they got published and, I would humbly suggest, because some librarians preserved them for later, more responsive readers.

Closely related to this shared concern is our mutual effort to promote reading. I presume such a stance hardly needs defending in this company—the value of reading skill in opening up the world of ideas, information, learning, and esthetic pleasure and pastime is a given among those who are themselves readers. We would pretty unanimously agree with Richard Mitchell's observation in his *The Graves of Academe* that "literacy is like the kingdom of Heaven. Those who seek it will find that other things are added unto them" [4, p. 158]. But an odd thing is happening to both of us these days: the competition of the media and other activities for the time once given to reading is beginning to loom as a threat which neither of us can ignore. As a result, both publishers and librarians have felt forced to widen the scope of their attention. We have not, as some groups have, abandoned the book and print, but we have begun to recognize the existence of other media and the potential values they represent in areas where once only print could have met the need.

What faces us both, and maybe begins to pull us apart, is the fact that the very concepts with which we identify are being changed by changing times. Think only of the words by which we have lived until now. "Publishing," for example, no longer means simply the production of printed materials. One need only look at the changes in content, format, and focus of attention in *Publishers Weekly*, with a regular section devoted exclusively to "Computer Update"; and its department on "Bookselling and Marketing" frequently dominated by new developments for selling not books but "software." Clearly, from now on, we are going to have to specify "book" or "print" publishing if that is what we mean because the term "publishing" alone does not carry that restrictive meaning any more.

In the discussion following Lerner's paper [5], the question was raised about what the term "journal" means, now that the electronic journal no longer need exhibit the standard features that the term used to conjure up. Osburn's paper [6, p. 85] raises a similar question about the term "collection."

Even a word like "literacy" is now applied to activities in which the ability to read is not considered an essential qualification. As (or if) this trend continues, it may become more difficult for librarians and publishers to find a common ground. On the other hand, it could bring us closer together if we see ourselves as the responsible gatekeepers and the last guardians of a part of the communication tradition that must not be lost.

And Philipson raised a question about what a library is [7, p. 14]. Well, it is a term derived from the word for "book," but it no longer means a place of books only. A library of tapes, of films, of cheeses, hardly raises a single etymological eyebrow.

The major change agent in all of this is, of course, the New Technology, with all its attendant promises and threats which have been so eloquently described these past two days. Certainly, if there *is* going to be a paperless society, traditional publishing and librarianship will have to change in highly significant ways. I am secretly delighted by the fact that, from the publishers' standpoint at the moment, the popular market for the computer and its related gadgetry is moving in quite the opposite direction from that of a *paper*less society: the May 6, 1983, issue of *Publishers Weekly* carried reviews of 19 new titles dealing with the computer, all from recognized book publishers—and that was only a small sampling of those outmoded artifacts of paper and print in the traditional codex format, still in demand by those who use the machines in the keeping of records, the simplification of the production of manuscripts, the storage and retrieval of information, and the reproduction of paper copies.

Reproduction, ay, there's the rub. It is the easy multiplication of paper by anyone with a text in his hand that has led to the most serious rift yet between publishers and librarians, but I think we have, in our floor discussions at least, pretty well established that the abuses, by and large, have been perpetrated less by librarians than by faculty and students not under our control. Now it need only be said that the world it is a-changin', not least in the realm of the production, dissemination, and preservation of ideas; and this presents a challenge that publishers and librarians must face either separately or together.

What, then, sets us at odds? Coser spoke of the hybrid nature of publishing, and that may provide a key to most of the confusions to which I have referred. The split personality of both librarianship and publishing is mirrored in the subtitle of his book, *The Culture and Commerce of Publishing,* and I suggest that this combination of considerations, seen by many as mutually exclusive categories, helps to account for the on-the-one-hand/on-the-other-hand nature of any exploration of our common concerns. It is in the cultural aspects that we find our most common ground and in the commercial aspects that we have the least in common.

For example, in the Coser, Kadushin, and Powell book, there is a checklist of factors that are involved in the editorial decision to publish a book, based on formal interviews with editors and participant observations in publishing houses [1, p. 145]. What struck me immediately is how many of these influential factors are involved in the librarians' selection process for library purchase; Coser's list reads like an outline for a traditional library school course in Book Selection.

Where we do differ, invariably, is in those items related to the direct effects of the factor on profits: the probable cost of production (not an element in the library's consideration, although the resulting cost of the volume could be); the potential sale of rights; the commercial prospects of the book; the book's potential profitability in the first year; its long-term profitability; and the ease with which it can be promoted. These factors—which have little to do with the social value of the book's content and everything to do with whether it will repay the publisher's investment—are where we part company, not because librarians are more noble but because we do not have to face that problem. Our investment is of a different kind, based on getting the book in the hands of readers, not necessarily purchasers (a distinction with a very real difference).

I do not put this forward as an ethical judgment; "non-profit," as Eugene Garfield told the Information Industry Association meeting in 1972, "is not necessarily more moral" [8, p. 52]. Precisely because publishers do have to worry about these matters, librarians do not—and in the worst possible light, I suppose one could say that librarians are getting a free ride at the publishers' expense. (That is, indeed, the light in which many publishers and writers see the librarian's office: the repeated campaigns to introduce a public lending right, the additional subscription cost levied by many journals when the purchaser is a library, and the bitter quarrel over the interpretation of "fair use"—all make it clear that librarians are often seen as parasites on the publishing body, taking credit for its ideals without accepting the risks.)

Librarians, of course, do not see themselves that way. And many publishers share the librarians' view that all persons, at least in a democracy like that of the United States, should have the right of access to the information needed to support their participation as citizens in the society. The view that information, both in its data and nondata aspects, should be withheld from those who cannot afford to pay for it, is still seen as a disturbing interpretation of the democratic ideal, even by many who have chosen to enter the field of publishing, for reasons other than—or in addition to—the goal of making money.

One of the concerns about the changing technology in the information field, particularly for librarians, is this very fact that it may so increase the cost, or so concentrate the control of the sources, that information, which can and should benefit the entire society, will be available only for a price beyond the reach of many. Peter Urbach foresees the time when the interposition of the online vendor between the publisher and the librarian will present the librarian with the need to pass on the charge to the user, and while this may, indeed, prove to be inevitable, it is hard to reconcile with the longstanding American image of the free public library.

Praeger [9] is also concerned with the problems that rising costs introduce into the publishers' traditional approaches, but—if I read him correctly—he seems to see the librarians' dilemma as simply a rather flimsy excuse manufactured by librarians to justify their ripping off the publishers. I am overstating his case, of course, but so—I think—is he: rising costs are harmful to us both; they are not—believe me—a windfall for librarians. Had he recognized that many librarians are unable, rather than "unwilling," to buy all the titles and copies that would be desirable, I would have liked it better.

We begin to raise social questions far beyond the immediate concern over sales or circulation statistics when information bids fair to become a commodity affordable only to a few. The Freedom to Send Messages has its other side—the Freedom to Receive Messages—and there are those of us in both the publishing and library sectors of the communication complex who are concerned about that, too. When the threat comes from specific censorship, we stand together. When the threat comes from proprietary rights in the product, the library is perceived in a different context—of interest to the publisher as a part of the paying public, rather than as a member of the dissemination team.

It is this odd double position held by the library—both receiver and distributor—that complicates the issue. As part of the paying public, the library acts as an important support of certain types of publishing: scholarly and serious works from university presses, professional monograph publishers, learned societies, and many of the commercial houses that aim at a smaller audience outside of the major mass market. This is the aspect of the publishing industry which still retains some of the features of what Coser nostalgically—and with some reservation—refers to in his paper as the "golden days of the past" [10, p. 6].

The parallel with that golden age is most clearly recognizable, still, in the community of interests shared by the University library and the

University press. Both exist to serve scholars—and so, of course, do some commercial publishers. My point is that "for professional, scholarly and special audience books," as Coser says, "library sales . . . provide a floor on which a second level of sales through bookstores or direct mailing may be safely built" [1, p. 343]. In something of the same vein, Lerner identifies the purchasers of her society's publications as members and nonmembers [5, fig. 1], which includes a considerable proportion of libraries. Without that margin of safety, many of that kind of serious publications might not be published at all under the traditional organization of the publishing industry.

It is in this aspect of publishing that publisher and librarian most amicably meet and are most interdependent: in the support of publications that have much smaller potential audiences and thus pose a greater risk and gamble for the publisher. Philipson [7, p. 14] suggests that what the scholarly publisher and the research librarian have in common is their sense of seriousness about what they do. I agree, but I assume that when Philipson says "serious" he does not necessarily mean sober. The need for information is not limited to those who themselves generate information; wisdom comes from a variety of experiences, of which the experience of reading is certainly one, and it may include experiences that delight and amuse.

But the segment of the audience that does generate new knowledge is an important one. As Praeger points out, a published work often contributes to yet another work and thus to the increase of knowledge, which benefits us all. May I suggest that often it is the library that makes that creative collaboration possible, particularly when the first work is out of print and no longer on the market? It is when it is still in the market, of course, that we step on toes—but it is only while it is still in the market that the library can acquire it, for use and users when the market cannot any longer supply it. The problem is that the library provides it without direct charge, in competition with those who must exact a charge for it. I cannot deny that, but neither the publisher nor the librarian has yet been able to show precisely, as Lucker suggests [11], how often this happens as compared to the number of times that library patrons learn from the library about books they wish to buy, or that a book from the library leads readers then to purchase it for permanent reference, or motivates them to seek other books, on the topic or by the author, which they wish to own. Certainly when either one of us—the librarian or the publisher—makes a reader out of a browser, both of us eventually benefit. Exactly how it all balances out has not yet been successfully measured.

The library, on the other hand, provides that base of a fairly constant purchaser who could make the difference for many serious titles. Libraries, of course, do buy the best-sellers too, and in multiple copies, but they are a minor aspect of that kind of sales. Where the library, particularly the academic and research library, does lend a helping hand is in the stand against the absolute surrender to the sure seller and the big-profit items. I believe that there are many publishers who consider this aspect of their enterprise worth preserving.

I turn, once again, to Coser, Kadushin, and Powell: "The advantage of books as a medium is that they do not have to have mass appeal; . . . the book industry is highly segmented so that most publishing is not for the mass market" [1, p. 201].

Once more, I see a parallel with librarianship. Our common bond with the publishers is that highly flexible medium, the book; our shared concern is with the diversity of needs that can be met by different books for different purposes; our solution has been, in both fields, the segmentation which produces outlets responsive to the different needs and purposes.

Like the publishing outlets, libraries are organized in different ways in order to deal with a tremendous range of interests and levels of education represented by the possible users of ideas in print. And as other media have proved useful in meeting the needs of users, we both have broadened our scope to go beyond books to other formats which can supplement, complement, and—in some cases—maybe even replace the traditional book in its traditional form.

Many of my students, coming for the first time to the exposés of the incursion of the conglomerates into the publishing business, of the decline of the personal bookstore, of the increasing importance to publishers of best-sellers, of the sale of subsidiary rights to the mass-oriented media, et cetera, et cetera, are firmly convinced that publishers care only for blockbusters and the fast buck, whereas librarians care only for the dissemination of ideas and the promotion of the book of lasting value. But this view can hardly be sustained, unless one ignores the infinite variety that marks the fields of both publishing and librarianship. All publishing is not centered in the Gothic paperbacks, and all librarianship is not contained in a research institute serving advanced scholars. Librarians can pride themselves on the fact that they do try to select materials of lasting value for their collections—but they select them, after all, from the output of the publishers. Publishers and librarians alike must be responsive to the demands of the entire gamut of their patrons' tastes if they are to survive.

Still the key distinction—for profit versus nonprofit—seems to introduce a palpable difference into the context in which our mutual goals are approached. Perhaps if we substituted the concept of "support" for that of "profit," the conflict between the motives which move both of our fields could be considerably reduced. It need not be said, but one always feels obliged to confirm, that nothing is really free. Libraries cost money; the growing variety of materials and services costs money; even a nonprofit organization must be able to pay its own way. In publishing, however, the financial underpinning is more directly apparent; it is the sale of books that makes their continued production possible. Librarians are more indirectly dependent on the support of their constituents: if more people come into the library demanding service, they do not represent more income, although they do represent greater costs. So winning the loyalty of our users and gaining their recognition of our value become important, not in an immediate, specific sense but in a more generalized and abstract one. A best-seller simply eats into a library's book budget instead of increasing it, and to that extent, librarians are not so tied to the marketplace *as* a marketplace. They are tied, instead, to an intangible: the value that people (taxpayers) attach to services that librarians provide. It is not at the point of sale that our social value is confirmed, but later—when a bond issue gets on the ballot, or when the university's budget comes up for review.

In that sense, then, libraries are as tied as publishers are to the concept of "giving them what they want." The key difference is that the "them" is much more a matter of each one of them individually than of a large-scale audience for a single item. This does make a difference, but it is not nearly so different as the idealist/realist dichotomy would lead us to believe.

Publishers, too, have the individual-item problem, as Coser's paper points out; each book has to make its own way, and (except for some real blockbuster writers with a large audience of ready-made readers) blanket approaches in advertising and guaranteed brand loyalty do not operate here as they do for most manufactured items. The librarian is at an even further remove from the mass-consumer market operation, but if we construct a continuum from the most profit-oriented to the least profit-oriented, book publishing would likely fall much closer to the library than to Nabisco on that scale.

What we do have in common is readers—a very special brand of human beings who, even when seen as consumers, cannot so reliably be counted on to act in conformity with group norms and actuarial averages. My guess is that, despite the frustrations that this phenomenon brings to us both, publishers and librarians are in the business they are in because they see a value—beyond financial profit—in serving that kind of individual human need.

It is because I believe this to be so that I side with those who feel that the new technological developments could eventually serve to bring publishers and librarians to a recognition of their common cause and their need to work together. The New Technology has already altered operations in both our occupations. Already some standard tools of our trade are online; already some of our information functions are being taken over by information brokers, a phenomenon sufficiently significant to have led to the establishment in 1982 of an Independent Librarians Group within the American Library Association, for those librarians now providing reference services in independent entrepreneurial situations. There is no question that many of the services performed by some of these newly created occupations do what librarians have always done but now do them more quickly and with more pizzazz than we did; for those who can afford to spend the money but do not wish to spend the time, buying these services from the new entrepreneurs provides many advantages with which our traditional means may not be able to compete.

But all of the implications of these shortcuts and new tools have not yet been examined or demonstrated. I am not quite so pessimistic as Praeger. There are some kinds of research, some uses of sources, some subject needs and processes that are not served solely by quantity and speed. I do not see even today's generation, for whom Pac-Man was babysitter, turning to their home computers when they want to read *Moby Dick* or even *Blue Highways*, McNeill's *The Pursuit of Power* or most of the publications from the kinds of presses, large and small, represented by the publishers who have spoken in this conference. Electronic publishing may well usurp the role played by loose-leaf, update services; compendia of quick-answer reference information; and many current indexes, union lists, catalogs, and bibliographies. Werner Mark Linz, in the "My Say" column of *Publishers Weekly*, says very well what I want to say: that the electronic media industry provides "the sensory stimuli, the facts and raw data," while the book publishing community provides "the interpretation, the continuity. . . . The first is concerned with the here and now, . . . the second is concerned with long-term significance" (what Philipson means, I would guess, by his term "seriousness") [12]. In other words, *The Guinness Book of World Records* could easily be replaced by an online data bank, but not *Remembrance of Things Past, Mr. Sammler's Planet,* or *The Color Purple.*

A certain responsibility rests with those of us who represent the tradition—the culture—of communication: to discover before it is lost that which is still needed, over and beyond what the machine is capable of providing. To retain the best of both the old and the new is part of the gatekeeper/guardian function that publishers and librarians share, and, as always in the cultural aspect of our occupations, the responsibility that is entailed is not just to our own self-preservation but to the preservation of societal values. In the face of some recent, immediate pressures, publishers and librarians have frequently found themselves in confrontation, voicing recriminations that have harmed us both. But the real point is that they have harmed not only us; they could harm values and needs that far transcend our problems of turf and title.

It is in this context—of our mutual commitment to the service of the society—that a dialogue should be carried out. It would be gratifying if this conference marked a first step toward the accomplishment of that purpose.

REFERENCES

1. Coser, Lewis A.; Kadushin, Charles; and Powell, Walter W. *Books: The Culture and Commerce of Publishing.* New York: Basic Books, 1982.
2. Drury, Francis K. W. *Book Selection.* Chicago: American Library Association, 1930.
3. Henderson, Bill. "The Small Book Press: A Cultural Essential." In this issue.
4. Mitchell, Richard. *The Graves of Academe.* Boston: Little, Brown & Co., 1981.
5. Lerner, Rita G. "The Professional Society in a Changing World." In this issue.
6. Osburn, Charles B. "Issues of Structure and Control in the Scholarly Communication System." In this issue.
7. Philipson, Morris. "Intrinsic Value versus Market Value." In this issue.
8. Doebler, Paul. "IIA Discusses the Copyright Dilemma." *Publishers Weekly* 202 (July 24, 1972): 52.
9. Praeger, Frederick A. "Librarians, Publishers, and Scholars, Common Interests, Different Views: The View of an Independent Scholarly Publisher." In this issue.
10. Coser, Lewis A. "The Publishing Industry as a Hybrid." In this issue.
11. Lucker, Jay K. "Publishers and Librarians: Reflections of a Research Library Administrator." In this issue.
12. Linz, Werner Mark. "My Say." *Publishers Weekly* 223 (May 6, 1983): 92.

THE CONTRIBUTORS TO THIS ISSUE

LESTER ASHEIM: for biographical information, see *Library Quarterly* 45 (January 1975): 73. Recent publications include "Trends in Library Education—U.S.A.," in *Advances in Librarianship* (New York: Academic Press, 1975), 5:148–201, "Librarians as Professionals," *Library Trends* 27 (Winter 1979): 225–57, and "Ortega Revisited," *Library Quarterly* 52 (July 1982): 215–26.

MARY BIGGS: interim chair, Information Services, Bowling Green State University Libraries, Bowling Green, Ohio. For biographical information, see *Library Quarterly* 53 (January 1983): 55. Recent publications include "Women's Literary Journals," *Library Quarterly* 53 (January 1983): 1–25, editor, special "Women in Print" issue, *New Pages: News and Reviews of the Progressive Book Trade*, vol. 3 (Summer 1983), in press, and author of an article in that issue, "The Feminist Press as Revolutionary Coffee Klatsch."

LEWIS A. COSER: distinguished professor of sociology, State University of New York at Stony Brook, Stony Brook, New York. Born Berlin, Germany, 1913. Ph.D., Columbia University, 1954. Publications include "The Private and Public Responsibility of the American Publisher," in *The Responsibility of the American Book Community*, edited by John F. Cole (Washington, D.C.: Library of Congress, 1981), *Books: The Culture and Commerce of Publishing*, with Charles Kadushin and Walter W. Powell (New York: Basic Books, 1982), and *Introduction to Sociology*, edited by Robert K. Merton (New York: Harcourt Brace Jovanovich, 1983).

BILL HENDERSON: publisher, Pushcart Press, Wainscott, New York. Born Philadelphia, Pennsylvania, 1941. B.A., Hamilton College, 1963; graduate studies at Harvard and University of Pennsylvania. Publications include *His Son: A Child of the Fifties* (New York: W. W. Norton & Co., 1981), editor, *Pushcart Press: Best of the Small Presses* (Wainscott, N.Y.: Pushcart Press, annual since 1976), and editor, *The Art of Literary Publishing* (Wainscott, N.Y.: Pushcart Press, 1980).

RITA G. LERNER: manager, Marketing Services, American Institute of Physics, New York, New York. Born New York, New York, 1929. B.A., Radcliffe College, 1949; M.A., Columbia University, 1951; Ph.D., Columbia University, 1956. Recent publications include editor, with G. L. Trigg, *Encyclopedia of Physics* (Reading, Mass.: Addison-Wesley Publishing Co., 1980), "Communication Satellites," in *Telecommunications and Libraries* (White Plains, N.Y.: Knowledge Industry Publications, 1981), pp. 57–67, editor, with G. L. Trigg, *Concise Encyclopedia of Solid State Physics* (Reading, Mass.: Addison-Wesley Publishing Co., 1982), and "Primary Publication Systems and Scientific Text Processing," with T. Metaxas, J. T. Scott, P. D. Adams, and P. Judd, in *Annual Review of Information Science and Technology*, vol. 18, edited by Martha E. Williams (White Plains, N.Y.: Knowledge Industry Publications, in press).

Jay K. Lucker: Director of Libraries, Massachusetts Institute of Technology, Cambridge, Massachusetts. Born New York, New York, 1930. B.A., Brooklyn College, 1951; M.L.S., Columbia University, 1952. Publications include "Library Resources and Bibliographic Control," *College & Research Libraries* 40 (March 1979): 141–53, "The Impact of Evolving Library Systems on Scholarly Publishing," in *Society for Scholarly Publishing: Proceedings of the First Annual Meeting* (Boston: Society for Scholarly Publishing, 1979), pp. 85–86, and "Electronic Publishing and Libraries" and "Document Delivery and Research Libraries," in *Prospects for Improving Document Delivery: Minutes of the 101st Meeting of the Association of Research Libraries* (Washington, D.C.: Association of Research Libraries, 1983), pp. 11–15, 83–88.

Charles B. Osburn: dean and university librarian, University of Cincinnati, Cincinnati, Ohio. Born Pittsburgh, Pennsylvania, 1939. B.A., Grove City College, Pennsylvania, 1961; M.A., Pennsylvania State University, 1963; M.S., University of North Carolina, 1971; Ph.D., University of Michigan, 1978. Recent publications include *Academic Research and Library Resources: Changing Patterns in America* (Westport, Conn.: Greenwood Press, 1979), *Research and Reference Guide to French Studies*, 2d ed. (Metuchen, N.J.: Scarecrow Press, 1981), "Collection Development: The Link between Scholarship and Library Resources," in *Priorities for Academic Libraries*, edited by Thomas J. Galvin and Beverly P. Lynch (San Francisco: Jossey-Bass, Inc., 1982), pp. 45–54, and "Toward a Reconceptualization of Collection Development," *Advances in Library Administration and Organization* 2 (1983): 175–98.

Morris Philipson: director, University of Chicago Press. Born New Haven, Connecticut, 1926. Diplôme, University of Paris, 1947; B.A., University of Chicago, 1949; M.A., University of Chicago, 1952; Ph.D., Columbia University, 1959. His latest novel is *Secret Understandings* (New York: Simon & Schuster, 1983).

Frederick A. Praeger: publisher and president, Westview Press, Boulder, Colorado. Born Vienna, Austria, 1915. University of Vienna, 1933–38.

Ted Solotaroff: senior editor, Harper & Row Publishers, Inc., New York. Born Elizabeth, New Jersey, 1928. B.A., University of Michigan, 1952: M.A., University of Chicago, 1956. His latest novel is *The Red-Hot Vacuum* (Boston: David Godine, 1979).

Peter F. Urbach: president, Pergamon International Information Corporation, McLean, Virginia. Born London, 1935. B.S.E.E., Carnegie Institute of Technology, 1957; M.E.A., George Washington University, 1963; J.D., George Washington University, 1968.